CHRISTIAN ENCOUNTERS

D. L. MOODY

CHRISTIAN ENCOUNTERS

D. L. MOODY

KEVIN BELMONTE

THOMAS NELSON
Since 1798

NASHVILLE DALLAS MEXICO CITY RIO DE JANEIRO

Published in Nashville, Tennessee, by Thomas Nelson. Thomas Nelson is a registered trademark of Thomas Nelson, Inc.

Scripture quotations marked NIV are from HOLY BIBLE: NEW INTERNATIONAL VERSION®. © 1973, 1978, 1984 by International Bible Society. Used by permission of Zondervan Publishing House. All rights reserved.

Scripture quotations marked KJV are from the KING JAMES VERSION. Public domain.

Published in association with Rosenbaum & Associates Literary Agency, Brentwood, Tennessee.

Thomas Nelson, Inc., titles may be purchased in bulk for educational, business, fund-raising, or sales promotional use. For information, please e-mail SpecialMarkets@ThomasNelson.com.

Library of Congress Cataloging-in-Publication Data

Belmonte, Kevin Charles.
  D.L. Moody / by Kevin Belmonte.
    p. cm. — (Christian encounters)
  "Published in association with Rosenbaum & Associates Literary Agency, Brentwood, Tennessee"—T.p. verso.
  Includes bibliographical references.
  ISBN 978-1-59555-047-7
  1. Moody, Dwight Lyman, 1837–1899. 2. Evangelists—United States—Biography. I. Title. II. Title: Dwight Lyman Moody.
  BV3785.M7B34 2010
  269'.2092—dc22
  [B]   2010020125

Printed in the United States of America

10 11 12 13 14 HCI 6 5 4 3 2 1

"I got a treat last night. Moody sat up alone with me till near 1 o'clock telling me the story of his life. He told me the whole thing. A reporter might have made a fortune out of it. . . . I think very few know what he really is."

—HENRY DRUMMOND

"There never lived a man more thoroughly unconventional . . . he tormented the navigators in easy sailing."

—C. F. GOSS

"Revivals are, as we read elsewhere, cyclonic. They recur. Possibly, one is due. If so, society will have reason to be grateful if there arises a revivalist so sound in himself, so true to his faith, so human in his contacts . . . as D. L. Moody."

—*THE NEW YORK TIMES*

"In an age of great preachers, [D. L. Moody] was perhaps the tallest and most mighty among them . . . he toured the U.S. and England, giving his solution to the gigantic crossword puzzle of the universe."

—*TIME* MAGAZINE

"You know the world is after peace; that's the cry of the world. That is what the world wants. Probe the human heart, and you'll find down in its depths a want, a cry for rest. Where can rest be found? Here it is, right here. Put your trust in the living God, with all your heart, mind, soul, and strength, and you'll have peace."

—D. L. MOODY

"Love is the lever with which Christ lifts the world."

—D. L. MOODY

To John Pollock, a treasured friend and guiding inspiration—and to my son, Sam, for whom D. L. Moody is already a friend.

CONTENTS

PROLOGUE

The Streets of Little Hell

In the late 1850s, when Charles Dickens was writing his greatest novels, an American version of *Oliver Twist* was playing itself out on the mean streets of Chicago. D. L. Moody was at the center of it.

It was all captured in a color lithograph of the time. Distributed nationwide, it called attention to the plight of ragged children from a slum in Chicago known as "Little Hell." They were the untouchables of this young and burgeoning city.[1] Moody, a child of poverty himself, had gone into their desolate world to provide wood or coal for their rude hearths, to provide food where it was needed, and to share the good news that had so changed his life—news he hoped would change theirs. He told them of Christ, whose love for the hungry, the poor, and those in need of shelter was the source of all he sought to do for them.

The names of the boys pictured in the lithograph sound as though they were lifted from Dickens's cautionary tale— Smikes, Red Eye, Billy Blucorn, Jackie Candles, and Darby the Cobbler.[2] But while the fortunes of Oliver Twist unfolded in vivid prose upon the printed page, Moody's work was writ large in the lives of real and desperately needy children.

A vignette from these years survives from the pen of William Reynolds, who then visited Moody and witnessed his work firsthand:

> The first meeting I ever saw him at was in a little old shanty that had been abandoned by a saloon-keeper. Mr. Moody had got the place to hold the meetings in at night. I went there a little late; and the first thing I saw was a man standing up with a few tallow candles around him, holding a negro boy, and trying to read to him the story of the Prodigal Son and a great many words he could not read out, and had to skip. I thought, "If the Lord can ever use such an instrument as that for His honor and glory, it will astonish me."
>
> After that meeting was over Mr. Moody said to me, "Reynolds, I have got only one talent; I have no education, but I love the Lord Jesus Christ, and I want to do something for Him; and I want you to pray for me."[3]

When Moody spoke to these children, his speech was riddled with contractions, errors of grammar, and rustic proverbs—all delivered in an unmistakably Yankee accent. Listen to one recording made of him speaking (shortly before his death), and one cannot fail to notice the countrified twang present in his pronunciation of the words *mercy* (rendered "mussy"), and *heart* (rendered "haat").[4] To the midwestern ears of his often unruly class, it must have seemed he spoke a language a little less foreign than the dialects heard among their German, Scandinavian, and Irish parents and relations.

What came through no less clearly than Moody's countrified speech was his love for the children of Little Hell. By 1860, his hardscrabble school had long since outgrown the shanty that was its first home and moved to a "great grimy hall"[5]—the North Market Hall—that was only an improvement so far as its ability to accommodate more ragged children was concerned.

And so it was that on the afternoon of Sunday, November 25, 1860, a VIP visited this Chicago school unlike any other— filled to the bursting with children (often a thousand or more) who were the poorest of the poor.

The scene that met his gaze must have been an eye-opener, beginning with the twenty-three-year-old teacher—looking slightly disheveled in "a checkered suit of gray clothes."[6] He was, in point of fact, not so very different from his students— raised as one of nine children by a widowed mother. Many had shaken their heads when he started his "school" in the abandoned saloon that served as its first meeting place. But he had persevered. He had brought them food, sometimes clothes, perhaps a piece of candy or the offer of a ride upon the pony he rode. They followed him to classes often described as barely contained bedlam—but they (and their parents) knew he cared. In a place where hunger, squalor, and abuse were rife, that counted for much.

Moody's VIP guest had agreed to visit the North Market Hall school provided he was not asked to speak. But Moody, prone to impulsive behavior, rather rudely seized the moment following the cheers with which his guest was greeted to good-naturedly force the issue. Our guest, he said, "has come to see the school on condition that *he not be asked to speak*. But if he wishes to say a word before leaving, we all have our ears open."[7]

There was little else for Abraham Lincoln to do but walk to the center of the room that housed this makeshift school and give a parting word. It was to be the only meeting of the one-time Yankee shoe salesman and the Illinois rail-splitter—a meeting as rich in symbolism as it was memorable. Two men with little formal education, two men who had known poverty in their youth, two men who would one day be remembered for having achieved great things.

Lincoln was near the top rung of a ladder he had long been climbing. His first election as president was a watershed moment in his life. There would be other and more transcendent moments to follow; but to this point it was a capstone experience.

Moody was not so very different from the young man Lincoln had been upon his arrival in New Salem, Illinois, as a twenty-two-year-old in April 1831—rough around the edges, but with latent gifts, a teachable heart, and a deep vein of sympathy for others.

What is most striking about Moody and Lincoln's meeting is that it reveals yet one more way in which they were alike. Moody had been drawn to the children of Little Hell because he saw something of himself in them. If they were fatherless, he had been fatherless too. If they were poor, he had known poverty. If they experienced loneliness and pain, he had endured that as well.

Lincoln's thoughts, when impudently pressed by Moody to make an impromptu speech, ran in the same channel. He looked out over the small sea of dirty faces before him, paused, and remembered. His remarks were brief, but as he spoke he evoked the memories of his own childhood and his words became poignant. He was president-elect of the United States, but he had not forgotten where he had come from:

> I was once as poor as any boy in this school, but I am now President of the United States, and if you attend to what is taught you here, some of you may yet be President of the United States.[8]

No one could have predicted what Lincoln and Moody would each give to their nation. Lincoln led America through the crucible of civil war. Moody, who spearheaded relief efforts for soldiers on both sides of that conflict, never wavered in his commitment to education or the poor. After the Civil War, the man once derided as "crazy Moody" came to be known as "the children's friend"—founding schools that still exist today and bringing the good news he had once shared among children in Chicago's slums to more than 100 million people.[9] But for a moment in 1860, when all that they would give lay in the future, the lives of these two men touched. Both left the world better than they found it.

1

THE FATHERLESS AND
THE WIDOW

Underlying it all was the New England landscape, that
varied and haunting beauty of rolling hills with their
spring and autumn splendor . . . best of all [was] the
river itself, flowing forever, like human life, out of
mystery into mystery. Even if his boyhood was not very
conscious of these things, they got hold of Moody and
kept hold of him all his days.[1]

—Gamaliel Bradford

When asked about his family heritage, D. L. Moody
once replied: "Never mind the ancestry! A man I
once heard of was ambitious to trace his family to
The Mayflower—and he stumbled over a horse-thief."[2]

One could be forgiven for thinking this witty, disarm-
ing quip more reminiscent of Mark Twain than someone
now regarded as the greatest evangelist of the nineteenth

century—but that was D. L. Moody—a man whose great good humor accounted in no small measure for his winsome faith.

From boyhood, Moody retained the puckish side of his personality—a remarkable thing in itself. For if his was in so many ways an eventful and celebrated American life, the story of his earliest years reads like the text of a New England tragedy.

Four-year-old Dwight Moody had only just begun to attend school when, on May 28, 1841, a neighbor poked his head in at the window of the schoolhouse in Northfield, Massachusetts, and asked if any of Ed Moody's children were there. Their father, the man said, had just died. Coming home, complaining of a great pain in his side, the rugged stonemason had staggered to his bedside and collapsed.

We know nothing of the sad and hurried return home Ed Moody's children endured, nor any details of the scene that met them when reunited with their grief-stricken mother, Betsy. All that remain are two stark but telling descriptions Moody gave in later life: "The first thing I remember is the death of my father. It was a lovely day in [May] when he fell suddenly dead. The shock made such an impression on me, young as I was, that I shall never forget it. I remember nothing about the funeral, but his death has made a lasting impression upon me. After my father's death the creditors came and took everything."[3]

And the second: "I had been in this world only three or four years when my father died bankrupt, and the creditors came and swept away about everything we had."[4]

"It brings the tears to my eyes [when] I think of it," Moody recalled many years afterward. "We had a hard struggle . . . My mother . . . cried herself to sleep at night."[5]

Little Dwight's grief was profound, and the pain he felt over the loss of his father seems never to have left him. In later years there is every indication that his experiences as a father caused poignant memories to resurface. "I shall ever remember one of [Mr. Moody's] illustrations," a friend recalled. "He had told one of his children that he was not to be disturbed in his study, and after a little while the door of the study opened and the child came in. 'What do you want,' [he said], and the little fellow looking up into his father's face said, 'I just wanted to be with you,' and the tears started into the great evangelist's eyes."[6]

Even as the pain of his father's sudden passing persisted, young Dwight was also troubled by a lingering fear of death.

> I well remember how in my native village in New England it used to be customary, as a funeral procession left the church, for the bell to toll as many times as the deceased was years old.
>
> How anxiously I would count those strokes of the bell to see how long I might reckon on living! Sometimes there would be seventy or eighty tolls, and I would give a sigh of relief to think I had so many years to live. But at other times there would be only a few years tolled, and then a horror would seize me as I thought that I, too, might soon be claimed as a victim by that dread monster. Death.
>
> Death and judgment were a constant source of fear to me.[7]

In the aftermath of Edwin Moody's passing, one crisis followed hard upon another. "My mother," Dwight remembered, "was left with a large family of [seven] children. One calamity after another swept over the entire household. [A month after my father's death] twins were added to the family, and my mother was . . . taken sick."[8]

Members of Betsy Moody's extended family rallied to her, nursing her till she recovered, helping to put food on the table. Her brothers in Boston helped her to pay the interest of the mortgage on her home, which consisted of "a little farmhouse and a few acres of stony ground on a hillside just [outside] the limits of the town."[9]

Counseled by some to break up her family and let others rear them, she refused, saying: "Not as long as I have these two hands."

"One woman cannot bring up seven boys," she was admonished. "They will turn up in jail, or with a rope around their necks."[10] Such Yankee straight talk fell on deaf ears. Betsy Moody would not yield.

As it happened, her determination was well founded. She knew something her well-meaning neighbors didn't—she had relations like her brother Cyrus, whose kindness during the first dark days after Edwin Moody's death was long remembered. Young Dwight never forgot one morning when he and the other children had been told to stay in their beds until school-time because they had no wood for a fire to heat their home: "I remember just as vividly as if it were yesterday, how I heard the sound of chips flying, and I knew someone was chopping wood in our wood-shed, and that we should soon have fire. I shall never forget Uncle Cyrus coming with what seemed to me the biggest pile of wood I ever saw in my life."[11]

Despite the kindness of Uncle Cyrus and other members of Betsy Moody's family, another bitter experience soon followed the death of her husband. Dwight never forgot it:

> The next thing . . . was that my eldest brother [Isaiah], to whom my mother looked up to comfort her in her loneliness and in her great affliction, all at once left home and became a wanderer. He . . . was seized with the belief that all he had to do to make his fortune was to go away, and away he went. I need not tell you how my mother mourned . . . how she longed and waited day by day and month by month for his return. Night after night she watched and wept and prayed. . . . Many a time we were told to go to the post-office to see if a letter had not come from him. . . . Many a time I have waked up in the night and heard her pray, "Oh, God, bring back my boy!"
>
> We would huddle together around the fire on an evening and ask her to tell us about our father, and she would talk for hours about him. But if the name of our eldest brother was by chance mentioned, then all would be hushed, for she never spoke of him except with tears. She would try to conceal them, but in vain. I used to think she loved him better than all of us put together, and I believe she did. When Thanksgiving Day would come she used to set a chair for him, thinking he would return home. Her friends and neighbors gave him up, but mother had faith to believe she would see him again.[12]

As Betsy Moody was grieving the loss of her eldest son, an unlooked-for grace entered her life in the person of the Reverend Oliver Everett of the Northfield Unitarian Church. Alone among her friends, he urged her "not to part with [her] children, but keep them together as best she could."[13] What is more, he promised to help.

He proved as good as his word. And though his pastoral compensation was modest at best, provisions from his larder were continually sent to the Moody household. He befriended Betsy and her children, modeling kindness for each of them. As W. H. Daniels wrote: "True to his promise, Pastor Everett used to help the widow [Moody] in the care of her children. He would visit them betimes, cheer them up with some pleasant words, settle quarrels among the boys, give the little ones a bright piece of silver all round, and bid the mother keep on praying, telling her God would never forget her labour of love. At one time he took little Dwight into his family to do errands and go to school."[14]

Betsy Moody warmed to this compassionate man. Several weeks after Edwin Moody's funeral, Everett baptized her and all her children "in the name of the Father and of the Son and of the Holy Ghost."[15] This was somewhat out of the ordinary, as Everett was a Unitarian. He appears to have been a Unitarian largely in name only, however, as he was quite orthodox in his beliefs concerning the central tenets of Christianity. He "believed in the Bible as the inspired word of God, in Jesus Christ as the Saviour of all sinners . . . in the Sabbath, and in the church and its sacraments."[16]

Young Dwight Moody was little less fond of Everett than

his mother was, and the depth of the affection he bore for the old pastor was revealed in the days following the appointment of a successor. The new pastor was a man in whom the milk of human kindness had run dry. Dwight could not remember "that the minister ever said a kind thing to me, or ever once put his hand on my head" in a gesture of kindness. "I don't think that he ever noticed me."[17]

Everett's successor undid much, if not all, of the good work Everett had invested in the Moody family, especially where Dwight was concerned. He now began "to look upon Sunday with a kind of dread,"[18] and soon ceased to have any interest in church at all.

But a hunger for fatherly kindness still persisted, revealed in one of Moody's most oft-repeated childhood stories.

It seems that several years after his father's death, Moody's brother Luther had gone to the neighboring town of Greenfield, hiring out to do chores for people there. "He was so homesick," Moody remembered,

> that he was constantly writing for me to come. He wanted me so much that he wrote that he would come home for me. I said I wouldn't go. But one cold day in November—I have never liked November—my brother came home, and said he had found a good place for me, and I must go down and spend the winter in Greenfield.
>
> I said I wouldn't go. But as my mother and I sat by the fire she said: "Dwight, I think you will have to go. I don't think I shall be able to keep the family together this winter."

It was a dark night for me. But mother's wish was enough. If she said I ought to that settled it. I didn't sleep much that night. I cried a great deal. The next morning after breakfast I took my little bundle and started. I was about ten years old.[19]

Moody joined his brother in Greenfield, but the happiness of their reunion was short-lived. He grew more homesick than Luther. At length, he said:

"Brother, I'm going home."

"What are you going home for?"

"I'm homesick."

"You'll get over it if you stick it out."

"No, I won't. I don't want to get over it. I can't stand it. I don't like those people here, anyway."

"Dwight, come out and take a walk with me," my brother said. He took me out near the courthouse square, led me to some shop windows, and showed me some jackknives. My eyes were full of tears. I didn't care for these things.

"I'm going home," I said.

All at once my brother, who was looking ahead, brightened up and said: "There comes a man that will give you a cent."

"How do you know?"

"Why," he said, "he gives a brand-new cent to every new boy that comes to town, and he will give you one."[20]

He was a feeble, white-haired man, and I was so afraid that he would pass me by that I planted myself directly in his path. As he came up to us my brother spoke to him, and he stopped and looked at me.

"Why, I have never seen you before, you must be a new boy," he said.

He asked me about my home, and then, laying his trembling hand upon my head, he told me that, although I had no earthly father, my Heavenly Father loved me, and then gave me a bright new cent. I do not remember what became of that cent, but that old man's blessing has followed me for over fifty years; and to my dying day I shall feel the kindly pressure of that hand upon my head.[21]

~

It was a bright moment amidst the hard work and struggle Dwight knew from the time that he could remember anything. A strong and sturdy little boy, he was set to work earning money early. "The first thing I did to earn money was to turn the neighbor's cows up on Strowbridge Mountain. I got a cent a week for it. . . . It was to go to mother [and] went into the common treasury."

One by one, Betsy Moody's children went to work, young as they were, and however modest the wage. "[When my brother] George got work, we asked who was going to milk the cows. Mother said she would . . . She also made our clothes, and wove the cloth, and spun the yarn, and darned our stockings."[22]

Such recollections create an impression that young Dwight Moody was a dutiful son, susceptible to kindness, yearning for fatherly affection, and often thoughtful and sensitive.[23]

All of these things are true. But it is no less true that as he grew older there were many times when he was a trial to his mother and others. W. H. Daniels, one of Moody's first biographers, took time and care to interview Moody himself, as well as various relations and close friends. Those he interviewed—including, it seems, Moody's mother—spoke with honesty and candor. The resulting portrait presents a young man who had many fine qualities but was in other ways a troubled and restlessly headstrong teen.

Moody's mother set the stage when she told Daniels: "He used to think himself a man when he was only a boy."[24] He "soon came to feel himself his own master." Strong, and taller than most (standing five feet ten inches when fully grown), he had "boundless ambition" and "a will strong enough to break down all opposition." For him, "anything was easier than submission."[25]

On the positive side "there were few things [Dwight] would not do for his mother: at her urgent entreaty he would even do a little studying."[26] That speaks well of him, since he had little inclination to study and heartily detested the local schoolmaster—"a man of violent temper, which he made no effort to control, and who severely used a rattan on the boys' backs upon the least provocation."[27]

Nearly all the time, there seems to have been a pitched battle in the little red schoolhouse, which stood almost opposite the house where the Moodys lived. "There were some bad boys who ran things," he remembered. "I was one of the worst."[28]

The consensus of friends and near relations was that young

Dwight was a bundle of contradictions. He would usually obey his mother, Daniels wrote,

> but she was the only person in all the world who ever was able to manage him. He was proud and wilful to the last degree, but full of generous impulses. He was ungovernable . . . Still there was nothing vicious in his disposition. If he could be made to see that he had wronged anyone, he was ready to beg his pardon for it, and do better . . .
>
> [Still] he was the leading spirit among the boys, and so much mischief did he lead them into that at length the teacher was in despair, and threatened to turn him out.
>
> At this his . . . mother was sorely grieved. She told him how . . . ashamed she should be to have one of her sons turned out of school, and directed him to go to the teacher, ask forgiveness for his bad conduct, and try to be a credit to his mother rather than a disgrace.[29]

Aside from his rather dismal performance as a student, Dwight was incurably fond of practical jokes. In this he was much like his contemporary Mark Twain, a boy whose intelligence and ability went long unrecognized and were masked beneath the conduct of a rabble-rouser. It was not unusual, for example, for Dwight to post a notice for a temperance lecture in the name of a noted speaker, only to draw a large crowd for a nonexistent event. He took pleasure in startling a farmer's horses, just as the hapless man was taking a drink, tipping him back into his wagon. When asked to give a public recitation of

Mark Antony's oration over Caesar's coffin during a "Closing School Exercises" night, Dwight agreed. He then hid a half-wild, yet silent kitten inside the coffin, and at the conclusion of his speech, he whacked the coffin hard, expelling the frightened, caterwauling creature amid screams that broke up the event.[30]

Near the end of Dwight's schooling, an unexpected influence entered his life when a new schoolmarm was appointed in place of the rattan-wielding schoolmaster. Dwight thought to make short work of her and broke up the class at the first opportunity to test her. He long remembered what followed:

> I was told to stay after school. I told the boys if [the teacher] tried the rattan on me there would be music.
>
> What do you think that teacher did? She sat me down and told me that she loved every one of the boys, and that she wasn't going to use the rattan on any one of them. If she couldn't teach school without whipping the boys she would resign. She spoke most lovingly and wept while talking.
>
> That broke me all up. I would rather have had a rattan used on me than to see her cry. I said, "You will never have any more trouble with me, and the first boy that makes trouble, I will settle him."
>
> That woman won me by grace. The next day one [of] the boys cut up, and I whacked him. I whacked him so much that the teacher told me that was not the way to win the boys.[31]

Like Winston Churchill in a later time, people close to Dwight Moody knew tears came often and easily to him. He never seemed ashamed of them. He felt deeply, honestly, and unaffectedly. And as the story of his encounter with his new teacher reveals, he could at times be brought to feel a keen and genuine remorse in ways that seemed decidedly at odds with his truculent nature.

≈

When Dwight Moody's years of formal schooling were done, he had gained the equivalent of a fifth-grade education.[32] His friend J. Wilbur Chapman commented on this:

> "A smattering of 'the three R's,' a little geography, and the practice of declamation made up the sum of his learning. . . . It was only during his last term that he began to apply himself with diligence, too late to make up for what he had lost. His reading is described as outlandish beyond description. With his characteristic tendency to jump directly to the heart of a question, he never stopped to spell out an unfamiliar word, but mouthed his sense of it without full dependence upon his training, or made up a new word which sounded to his ear as suitable as the original."[33]

Other elements were a part of the unbroken and coltish aspects of young Dwight's personality. J. C. Pollock, one of Moody's ablest biographers, wrote:

> Farm work was irksome . . . Dwight loved to be free on the hills. He loved to run, "and I could run like a deer;" to fight other boys; to swim, reveling in the cold water of the Great

River, to be the leader in practical jokes such as stampeding a farmer's cattle with Indian war whoops, or snowballing innocent riders.

By seventeen he was a broad, sloping-shouldered youth with plenty of muscle and stamina, of medium height growing to five feet ten, though a tendency to let his head hang forward as if to [sic] heavy for his body made him look stocky. His eyes were darkish gray, his hair rich brown, almost black. His lips had rather a pout. And the last joint of both little fingers had a crook inwards so that the tips rested on the next.

With the boys able to earn food cheap, firewood free, the crowded [Moody] family made the little frame house echo with laughter. But Moody hated hoeing fields and husking corn barefoot . . . Chopping wood against the snowbound winter was a dreary chore, and he was "sick and tired" of doing it all for nothing. He did not grudge his mother a penny but wanted money to spend on himself too.[34]

Young Moody's love of swimming appears to have led to a brush with death at or about this time. "I have twice been in the jaws of death," he recalled long years later. The event, of which he seems seldom to have spoken, left a lingering impression: "Once I was drowning, and as I was about to sink the third time I was rescued. In the twinkling of an eye it seemed as though everything I had said, done, or thought of flashed across my mind."[35]

Sobering as this experience may have been, it was—as is the way with so many young men—soon after subsumed by a wish to strike out on his own. So strong was this urge that it eventually overwhelmed even the ardent, steadfast devotion he felt for his mother. As his son Will Moody wrote: "While cutting and hauling logs on the mountain side with his brother Edwin one day in the early spring of 1854, [seventeen-year-old Dwight] exclaimed, in his characteristically abrupt manner: 'I'm tired of this! I'm not going to stay around here any longer. I'm going to the city.'"[36]

2

YOUNG MAN IN A HURRY

[Moody's] journey to Boston [was] in much the same mood as possessed Benjamin Franklin when he journeyed from Boston, [including] his adventures as a salesman in a retail shoe shop . . . [but most singular of all was] his conversion to Christianity by the mild eloquence of Edward Kimball.[1]

—*The New York Times*

When I first went to Boston I was what you might call a tramp; I was in that city without a place to lay my head.[2]

—D. L. Moody

Dwight Moody may have entered Boston much as Benjamin Franklin entered Philadelphia for the first time—and it is interesting to note that both were seventeen when they struck out on their own. Moody did indulge in some Franklinesque escapades during his time in Boston. But in other ways, the experience of the two men could hardly have been more different—especially when it came to matters of faith.

At the outset, Moody could not have cut a more nondescript figure when he stepped off a train in Boston in early April 1854.[3] Franklin remembered that he made "a most awkward, ridiculous appearance"[4] when entering Philadelphia; but he at least had some money in his pocket. Moody hadn't a penny to his name.

That he got to Boston at all was due to his elder brother George, who, like his mother, had been opposed to his going. Still, George had shown a brother's kindness, which Moody never forgot. Seeing that Dwight was determined to go—even if he had to walk the one hundred miles to get there—George met him halfway between their home and the depot and pressed five dollars into his hand.[5] It was just enough to cover a one-way fare. Once in Boston, the headstrong teen would truly be on his own, without money to purchase food or secure lodging.[6]

After arriving in Boston, Dwight, or "D. L.," as he now preferred to be called, wasted little time in getting to the prosperous shoe store owned by his mother's brother Samuel Holton.[7] It soon became apparent that the young man harbored hopes his uncle did not share. D. L.'s plan seems to have been to present himself at his uncle's store, whereupon he fully expected to be offered a position.

Such thinking had little basis in fact. When D. L. walked through the door, Uncle Samuel's reaction was a mixture of surprise, chagrin, and dismay. He now had a nephew on his hands who had given him no advance notice of his arrival. To make matters worse, Holton knew that his nephew was hard to handle. As an old New England phrase had it, "no one had been able to slap a saddle on him." This had become apparent when, at Thanksgiving dinner 1853, D. L. voiced an interest in coming to Boston. Uncle Samuel had said nothing, but talked to George Moody afterward, who urged his uncle not to take his brother on, "for in a short time, Dwight would want to run the store."[8]

Uncle Samuel took his nephew to the shoe store office, where they chatted pleasantly for a few moments about family doings. He then abruptly indicated he had no more time to visit and began to show D. L. to the door, asking the thunderstruck teen as they walked what he planned to do now that he was in Boston. Misplaced hopes began unraveling fast. D. L. heard himself say that he had come to find a position. Uncle Samuel said nothing. A few moments later D. L. was back out on the street, badly shaken, not knowing quite what had just happened. This was not at all what he had planned.[9]

Kindness then intervened in the person of Uncle Samuel's younger brother Lemuel, a partner in the shoe store. Uncle Lemuel may well have overheard D. L.'s conversation with Uncle Samuel, for he approached the boy and suggested he lodge with him and his family in their suburban Winchester home until he found work.[10]

Then followed two days that lingered ever after in D. L. Moody's memory. Forty years later, he could still vividly recall his feelings: "I remember how I walked up and down the streets trying to find a situation, and I recollect how, when [people] answered me roughly, their treatment would chill my soul . . . It seemed as if there was room for everyone else in the world, but none for me. For about two days I had the feeling that no one wanted me. I never have had it since, and I never want it again."[11]

Moody's friend J. Wilbur Chapman then picked up the story. After days of efforts and meeting nothing but failures, Dwight grew discouraged with Boston and told his uncle Lemuel he was going to New York. The uncle strongly advised against this and urged him to speak to his uncle Samuel again about the matter.

With boyish pride, he refused, saying his uncle Samuel knew perfectly well what he wanted. But Uncle Lemuel insisted. So D. L. asked his uncle Samuel for a place in his store.

"Dwight," his uncle replied, "I am afraid if you come in here you will want to run the store yourself. Now, my men here [need] to do their work as I want it done. If you want to come in here and do the best you can, and do it right, and if you'll ask me when you don't know how to do anything, or if I am not here, ask the bookkeeper, and if he's not here, one of the salesmen or one of the boys—and if you are willing to go to church and Sunday school when you are able to go anywhere on Sundays, and if you are willing not to go anywhere at night or any other time which you would not want me or your mother to know about—why, then, if you'll promise all these things, you may come [and] we'll see how we can get along. You can have till Monday to think it over."

"I don't [need to wait] till Monday," Dwight said, "I'll

promise now." And so it was that a chastened young man began to work in his uncle's shoe store.[12]

Moody needed taking in hand, and however reluctantly Samuel Holton might have come to it, he deserves credit for coming to his nephew's aid. As subsequent events would prove, his no-nonsense brand of tough love set in motion a series of events that would begin to reveal the diamond-in-the-rough qualities Moody possessed, leading ultimately to the young man's conversion to Christianity.

It was an eventful new life nearly from the start. Boston was a city of some 150,000 people when D. L. Moody arrived there in April 1854. Less than seventy-five years removed from its days as a British colonial capital, there was an old-world, cultured air about the place—cobblestone streets, handsome brick buildings, and many sites that evoked the history of two centuries and more.

At the same time, Boston was a magnet for immigration and commerce, replete with foreign dialects from many corners of the world.[13] This side of city life filled one of D. L.'s first letters home to his family, spelled phonetically and rife with errors in grammar, but rich in images of his life and experiences. "A steam hot gas ship come in," he wrote in a letter to his brothers on April 9, "and sutch a site I never seen before. There was a ship from Liverpool loaded with emegrans. All the Greeks in Boston was there. The sailors sung a song when they come in site of their friends. Sutch meetings as there was there, I never see."[14]

During his first few days in Boston, Moody had taken in sights when he could, discovering things unlike any he had ever known. He told his brothers, for example, that he had come across "three great building[s] full of girls, the handsomest there is in the city, thuy all swor like [pirates]."[15]

But such moments as these were brief interludes in a life now dominated by hard work.[16] Determined to prove himself as a shoe salesman, he now went at it in every way he could think of. As his son Will later wrote:

Moody was learning to be a salesman and he rapidly became proficient. Conventional but unfruitful methods he discarded, and adopted others more aggressive. When the window display failed to attract customers, he did not hesitate to embrace the medieval practice of accosting passers-by with an invitation to enter the store and examine the goods. Soon he induced his employer to permit him to forego holidays and share the profits gained by keeping the shop open when other places of business were closed. On such occasions there was always a large number of country visitors only too glad to find they could combine necessary trading with a pleasure trip to the city.[17]

Still, Moody found his new conditions irksome at times.

The love of mischief would again assert itself. On one occasion the cobbler was the victim of the youthful clerk. Moody carefully made a little slit with a sharp knife in the leather seat of the bench. He placed beneath this a pan of water so that when the occupant placed his weight on it, the small aperture opened and the water beneath came through. The mystified cobbler only discovered the secret of his annoyance by [Moody's] ill-concealed [laughter].[18]

After a long day's work in the little store, Moody would often take exercise by running around Boston Common, often taking time for pranks. Once, he walked up to a stranger and, without a word of greeting, silently accompanied him. Matching his gait to that of the stranger, he continued to walk until the Boston citizen, thoroughly convinced that the youth was demented, fled.[19]

"From a daybook," Will Moody wrote, "with entries from July 1, 1854, to June 4, 1856, there are items against the name of D. L. Moody indicating that his salary was small. He had already been in his uncle's employ for over a year before any credit entries appeared, apparently indicating that during this period his wages were sent directly to his mother. From June 1856 to September his total payments were but $57.28."[20]

At the same time, Moody began to pursue a course of self-improvement. True to his word, he began to attend church services at the Mount Vernon Congregational Church, which his uncle Samuel attended. He became involved in the kind of social groups of which his uncle approved, and D. L. wrote about this to his brothers:

I went to Sunday school in the morning, and then I went to one this noon; but I don't belong to only one. I am going

to join the [Young Men's] Christian Association tomorrow
night. Then I shall have a place to go to when I want to go
anywhere. And I can have all the books I want to read free
from expense. Only have to pay one dollar a year. They have
a large room, and the smart men of Boston lecture to them for
nothing, and they get up and ask questions. The place where I
board, there are about twenty-five clerks and some girls. We
have a jolly time.[21]

Among the "smart men" whom Moody might have heard
lecture, some are still well known today. He could hardly have
chosen a better or more advantageous time to sample the life of
the lyceum culture, then so prevalent. J. C. Pollock described
this time in Moody's life:

Moody went to . . . lectures, having quickly discovered that to
be a smart clerk he must not only read books but learn from
the learned. Almost certainly he would have laughed with
Oliver Wendell Holmes, who loved lecturing. He may have
heard Longfellow declaim . . . The Boston neighborhood in
1854 teemed with intellectual life. Any day Moody might
sell shoes to Emerson or Lowell, Dana or Whittier or Julia
Ward Howe, or those cultured young Bostonians, Henry and
William James and Phillips Brooks.[22]

But not all Moody's activities were innocent or in the nature
of approved behavior. When out of earshot or away from
Uncle Samuel's watchful eye, he was still very much a young

man who could be "immature, inexperienced and crude."[23] He was drawn to excitement and witnessed or involved himself in things he never forgot—an accidental explosion on Boston Common, and a terrible fire at Sargent's Wharf. But by far his most wrenching and dramatic experience involved the riots that ensued on May 24, 1854, when abolitionists attempted to prevent the extradition of the fugitive slave Anthony Burns to the southern states.[24]

As it happened, the old courthouse where Burns was being held was opposite the shop in which Moody worked. The sight of this man being carried through the street in chains seems to have angered him, and he briefly joined the mob who threatened to free the prisoner forcibly—a mob who only dispersed "when shots were fired over the heads of the people."[25]

At this point, Moody appears to have ducked and run, retreating to relative safety of "a precarious perch over the Holton store." What happened next is related in his own words:

> I got up in to the secont story right over our [awning] and thare I stade un till it was over with. All the compineys was out and thare was all of 35 difrent compineys. George Beans and my self got up there a bout 10 aclock and thare we sat un till 3 in the afternoon. Thay tock him out a bout 2:30 to such groaning and hising you never hird. I was all burnt up in the son the polis came up to the store when he was clearing the street and told us to com down. But we was up so he could not reach us . . . He told us to come down the secont time, but we would not com. So he at to let us be and so I see it all.[26]

Moody had seen Boston in ferment, and been caught up in it. But not all was high drama or tragedy. There were moments of leisure when he could get out in the open spaces of Boston Common, running hard around its perimeter in the summer, swimming in the Charles River, and eating as many black mince "slugs" and apple "doughbats" as his pocket money allowed.[27]

In the winter months, he might join in toboggan runs that would often as not end in a fight. In such moments all of his coarse habits would come on in a rush. "I used to have a terrible habit of swearing," he remembered. "Whenever I would get mad, out would come the oaths."[28]

And always, there was his love of practical jokes. "I was full of animal life," he recalled,

> and shut up in the store through the day, and sleeping there at night, I had to have some vent, and used to lie awake at nights to think of some new joke to play upon somebody. My first victim was the cobbler employed in the store. He was an Italian . . . and although he liked me, he had such an awful temper that my joking him came near costing my life.
>
> One day I fitted a lady with an expensive pair of shoes and he was changing the buttons when enraged by some trick I played upon him he took his knife and cut the shoe he held into pieces. Another time—and this was the last trick I played upon him—he seized the knife and sprang at me and for a few minutes I had all I could do to keep out of his reach.[29]

Still, "Moody had no regrets that he had left farming to be a salesman; instead of mucking unresponsive weeds he was persuading people, charming them, and molding their wills to buy more and costlier shoes. He reveled in the battle to trade better than the other clerks."[30]

≈

Meanwhile, despite all of the trial and error that was a part of his life, Moody continued to obey his uncle Samuel's wishes and attend the Mount Vernon Church. It was here that he met one of the most important people he would ever meet in his life: his Sunday school teacher, Edward Kimball.

Kimball, a man of sensitivity and tact, quickly learned that his new class member knew little of the Bible. Moody shared his class with young people who were students at Harvard. Rather than try to help Moody find his way when various passages were cited, they did little to hide their sense of amusement at his expense.[31] Kimball reproved them.[32] Long years later he recalled the incident:

> One Sunday [D. L. Moody] appeared in the Sunday school of Mount Vernon Church . . . He took his seat among the other boys. I handed him a closed Bible and told him the lesson was in John. [He] took the book and began running over the leaves with his finger [in the Old Testament] looking for John. Out of the corners of their eyes the boys saw what he was doing . . . I gave [them a] hasty glance of reproof . . . I [then] quietly handed Moody my own book, open at the

right place, and took his. I did not suppose [he had] noticed the glances exchanged between the other boys over his ignorance, but it seems . . . that he did, [for he later] said in reference to my little act in exchanging books that he would "stick by the fellow who had stood by him and had done him a turn like that."[33]

On other occasions Moody showed an increasing interest in the Scriptures that was artless in its sincerity. Often, he would sit though a class silently, taking things in. "But at times," his son Will said, "his interest would betray him," and he would jump in with comment or question.

So it was when Kimball began to describe the leadership and work of Moses as he guided the children of Israel in their wanderings. Something in Kimball's account seems to have captured Moody's imagination, for he interrupted and exclaimed: "Say, Mr. Kimball, that man Moses must have been *smart!*"[34]

Though Moody was untutored in the basics of the Christian faith, Kimball sensed that his young friend, for all of his rough edges, might be hearing the call of God to his heart. The more he thought and prayed about it, the more settled this conviction became. And so, on April 21, 1855, he decided to seek Moody out at his uncle's store. "I started down town to Holton's shoe store," he remembered.

When I was nearly there, I began to wonder whether I ought to go just then, during business hours. And I thought maybe my mission might embarrass the boy, that when I went away the other clerks might ask who I was, and when they learned [of my errand] might taunt Moody . . .

While I was pondering over it all, I passed the store without noticing it. Then when I found I had gone by the door, I determined to make a dash for it and have it over at once.

I found Moody in the back part of the store wrapping up shoes in paper and putting them on shelves. I went up to him and put my hand on his shoulder, and as I leaned over I placed my foot upon a shoe box. Then I made my plea, [though it seemed to me to be] a very weak one. I don't know just what words I used . . . I simply told [D. L.] of Christ's love for him and the love Christ wanted in return.

That was all there was of it, [though] Mr. Moody said afterward that there were tears in my eyes. It seemed that [he] was just ready for the light that then broke upon him, for there . . . in the back of that shoe store in Boston [he] gave himself and his life to Christ.[35]

"Many years afterward," wrote J. Wilbur Chapman, "Mr. Moody himself told [me] the story of that day. 'When I was in Boston,' he said,

"I used to attend a Sunday school class, and one day I recollect my teacher came around behind the counter of the shop . . . put his hand upon my shoulder, and talked to me about Christ and my soul. I had not felt that I had a soul till then. I said to myself: 'This is a very strange thing. Here is a man who never saw me till lately, and he is weeping over my sins, and I never shed a tear about them . . . I don't remember [exactly] what he said, but I can [still] feel the power of that man's hand on my shoulder.'"[36]

It was the watershed moment of D. L. Moody's young life, and his response to Kimball's plea was very much like his response years earlier to the teacher who had sought to win him through an act of kindness and love. What shone through clearly was that Kimball had a winsome and compelling testimony. The God and Savior of whom he spoke seemed to answer in themselves all of the most important questions D. L. had ever asked within the deep places of his heart. An eternal moment kindled within him, and he embraced the Christian faith.

Years later, Moody offered a description of his feelings at this time, striking in its tenderness and imagery. There was a kind of poetry in his words:

> I remember the morning I came out of my room after I had first trusted Christ, and I thought the old sun shone a good deal brighter than it ever had before; I thought that the sun was just smiling upon me, and I walked out upon Boston Common, and I heard the birds in the trees, and I thought that they were all singing a song for me.
>
> Do you know I fell in love with the birds? I never cared for them before; it seemed to me that I was in love with all creation. I had not a bitter feeling against any man, and I was ready to take all men to my heart.[37]

3

"A VERY LIVELY CITY"[1]

And we will see the Gospel going down into dark lanes
and dark alleys, and into dark garrets and cellars, and
[lost souls] come pressing into the kingdom of God.[2]

—D. L. Moody

Within five years of his arrival in Chicago in the
early autumn of 1856, D. L. Moody had achieved a
measure of success beyond anything he could have
imagined. By 1860, he had saved between seven thousand and
twelve thousand dollars.[3] One year later, at the age of twenty-
four, his annual income was in excess of five thousand dollars.[4]
"I was very ambitious to get rich," he wrote, "[to earn] one hundred thousand dollars . . . was my aim."[5]

According to the Census of 1850, the average annual
income for male workers in the trades was almost exactly three
hundred dollars.[6] Conservatively speaking, Moody was making

more than sixteen and a half times the annual wage of a tradesman in 1850.[7]

Back in Boston, Uncle Samuel would never have believed
it. Grateful for his nephew's conversion, and instrumental in it,
he had nonetheless become increasingly frustrated by a young
man who always seemed to be "a law unto himself."[8] By 1856,
D. L.'s success as a salesman was beyond dispute; but little else
about their relationship seemed to be.

A quarrel precipitated the final breach between them.
Its cause is not certain—it may be that D. L. demanded and
was refused a raise—though it is just as likely Uncle Samuel
objected to Moody's stated desire to go west in the near future
and demanded a signed agreement saying he would not. "Uncle
[Samuel] objected to my goin'," Moody wrote to his mother.
And in a letter to his younger brother Warren, he said, "I hope
you will never have anyone to cross your path . . . and blast
your hopes. I thought the quicker I went and got out of [Uncle
Samuel's] way the better."[9]

Moody's son, Will, despite a Victorian penchant for flowery
prose, seemed to put his finger on the nub of the problem: "For
some months [Father] had fretted under the conservative methods
of the business house in which he was engaged, and had longed to
enter a larger sphere of activity, and when a crisis finally came in
his relations with his employer, and there seemed little opportunity for advancement, he decided to go to Chicago."[10]

Upon his arrival in Chicago, Moody's ascent among the
ranks of young men out to do well for themselves was rapid.
Through the good offices of his uncle Calvin Holton (a resident

of Des Plaines),[11] he secured employment in Wiswall's boot and shoe store. His youngest son, Paul, wrote:

> Though personal appearances were still against him, his ability as a shoe salesman soon asserted itself. He became popular with the rougher class of customers, and used to take especial [pride] in handling difficult people
>
> After a time, when [Mr.] Wiswall added a jobbing department to his business, [Father] found himself still more in his element. It gave him a chance to push out in his own interests, to exercise his tireless energies outside the routine of the store. He used to visit the depots, and inspect the hotel registers for incoming visitors. When the store closed at night, he would accost passers-by and try to sell them rubbers or other seasonable goods. He was all the time on the lookout for customers.[12]

At nineteen, Moody was hitting his stride, and it was with no little feeling of self-satisfaction that he wrote to his youngest brother, Samuel, back home in Northfield, on December 16, 1856: "I suppose you would like to know how I am doing. Well, I am doing first-rate. [I] shall [visit home] in the summer, if not before." In a letter to his mother, written on the same day, he confided: "I have made thirty dollars a week ever since I came out here. Don't let Uncle Samuel get hold of it, but as it has turned out, I have done the very best thing in coming [west]."[13]

Moody was more right than he knew. He had no way of knowing, but when he attended the morning Sunday school in the First Baptist Church on the first weekend he was in Chicago, his future wife, Emma, sat there among the pupils, then a girl in her teens.[14]

≈

"[Mr. Moody's] heart had always been sensitive and tender," a friend once observed, and it was "natural for him to run to the assistance of any one in trouble."[15] More than any other description, this best describes why Moody took up Christian work among the children of Little Hell.

This chapter of his life unfolded gradually—a mirror of the work in progress of Moody as a person. Soon after his arrival in Chicago, he "joined the Young Men's Mission Band of the First Methodist Episcopal Church, whose purpose was to visit hotels and boarding houses on Sunday mornings, distributing tracts and inviting people to church services."[16]

But he was busy on Sunday afternoons as well. It was then he attended "a little mission Sabbath-school on the corner of Chicago Avenue and Wells Street." Enjoying his time there, and wanting to help, he soon offered to teach a class. Grateful as the school superintendent was, he told Moody that he had twelve teachers already and only sixteen students. "But," he said, "if you can work up a class of your own, you would be welcome."[17]

The following Sunday, Moody arrived with eighteen ragged and dirty children taken straight from the streets of the city. One can only imagine the superintendent's astonishment at seeing his entire school more than doubled in this way.

It is interesting that Moody had no thought of teaching these needy children himself. What he knew how to do was "drum up" recruits. This he did "until he filled the little school to overflowing."[18]

As he looked back on that first Sunday and the first eighteen children he had gathered, he felt a tremendous sense of satisfaction and fulfillment. "That was the happiest Sunday I have ever known," he said. "[I was two years] trying to find out what my work was before I succeeded. If I could not teach them, I could take them where there were those who could teach them."[19]

$\approx$

In the fall of 1858, when he was twenty-one, Moody decided on a radical step. He seems to have concluded on his own that not enough children were being helped. And so, rather than continue to ask children to come with him to the school on Chicago Avenue, he would go to them. That such a thing was wholly unheard of can be judged from the way some began to refer to him at this time—"crazy Moody."

He cheerfully ignored them.

Years later, one of Moody's "boys," Jimmy Sexton, described his first impressions of the man he came to know as a friend. Sexton (who became a colonel in the Union army[20]) found Moody to be funny, kind, and not at all put off by "our boyish chaffing"—saying it "pleased rather than annoyed him." Sexton and the other boys had, in a word, found a "new stranger friend" very much like themselves—rough, rowdy, and very much down to earth.[21]

Before Sexton knew what was happening, he and the other members of what was called "the gang" had more or less been drafted. The kind of coercion Moody used, however, was anything but forced. He invited Sexton and the other ragged boys to help him start a mission Sunday school—to be, as Sexton remembered, partners in "the whole thing."[22] For the first time in their lives, someone had taken an interest in them. They warmed to this man who seemed to be so much like themselves.

From the start, Moody threw convention to the winds. His first task was to commandeer an abandoned freight car on North State Street and start holding classes there.

But they were classes unlike any other. Passersby of the old freight car on successive Sunday afternoons might hear whoops, cheers, and a rousing song (more shouted than sung) like the newly written "Stand Up, Stand Up for Jesus." Briefly, one of Moody's coworkers might speak (no longer than two or three minutes), and then the whole sequence would begin again.

Moody himself still had not mustered the courage to speak to his boys—he really didn't know what to say—but in all other respects he was the ringmaster of this often raucous Sunday school.

Meanwhile, Jimmy Sexton and the other members of the gang were not idle. They rounded up other boys in ever increasing numbers until the old freight car was full to the bursting. One of Moody's church friends, Lawyer King, heard about the stir Moody's school had created and told D. L. that he knew of an abandoned saloon on Michigan Street. Rotting and ratty, it was nonetheless roomier than the freight car. In that sense it was an improvement; though just barely.[23]

What was unfolding with Moody's school and the children drawn to it in increasing numbers conjured memories that lasted on into the years. One Moody friend, a Chicago minister named G. S. F. Savage, recalled: "In this tumble-down old house he began to gather in the children. He went out into the streets with candy and knickknacks and got the good will of the children."[24] Lawyer King remembered: "All loved [Moody], because he took such an interest in their welfare. No one [forgot his] pleasant smile and . . . cordial handshake."[25]

Sunday events proved so successful that Moody opened the saloon for the first weeknights it had seen in years. Savage visited one evening and never forgot what he saw: "There were no gas fixtures in the house and [Mr. Moody] was trying to light it with half a dozen candles, but the darkness rather had the best of it. I found him with a candle in one hand and a Bible in the other, and a child on his knee who he was trying to teach. There were twenty-five or thirty children in all, and they were as sorry a lot of little ragamuffins as could have been found in Chicago."[26]

Savage's account, useful in many ways, is in one respect far too prim and Victorian to convey the sight that so often met Moody's eyes when he entered the world of Little Hell. The children he sought to help were far more than "a sorry lot of ragamuffins." Such descriptions have the effect of making Moody sound more like a pied piper than what he really was: someone extending a lifeline to hundreds of children at a point of crisis. Lyle Dorsett, one of Moody's finest biographers, has described their plight better than anyone: "These children were emotionally and physically wounded. Often beaten, sexually abused, malnourished, and exposed [to] drinking, [drug addiction], gambling, and prostitution, these youngsters were discarded and treated like rats and other vermin that roamed their wooden shanties and tenement hovels."[27]

Dorsett's description of what drew Moody to Little Hell is no less valuable:

> [He] entered [Little Hell] armed with a God-given confidence that he was to rescue the children. With only about three years of formal schooling, a reality that put him at a disadvantage in polite company, he found in Little Hell a place where his meager learning would not be noticed. Furthermore, Moody knew what it was like to live with only one parent, and he had experienced loneliness and poverty, if not the exposure to crime, physical abuse, and sexual degradation. [And so,] in 1858, Moody rented a vacant, decrepit saloon. He cleaned it up as well as he could and turned it into a "Sabbath School."[28]

Moody's Chicago friend W. H. Daniels penned another description of Little Hell:

> This was a section on the Lake shore, north of the river, which was to Chicago what the Five Points were to New York . . . or St. Giles's to London. It was a moral lazaretto.[29] Disorder,

and even crime, was regarded as a matter of course . . . which would have been checked and punished in any other part of the city. [But] this [was an] abandoned region . . . and it was proverbially dangerous for any decent person to walk those streets after nightfall. Thither went Moody to recruit his Sunday-school.[30]

Tenderness for these lost children seemed to consume Moody, as did the desire to bring something better into their lives. W. H. Daniels wrote that he had "an intense and almost womanly love for children. He never seemed happier than when in the midst of a crowd of boys and girls, with whom he romped in the wildest fashion, beating them at their own sports and games."[31]

Moody's work was also intensely practical. The poor parents of Little Hell (single or otherwise) often needed their children "to help buy food, clothing, and fuel for heat and clothing."[32] Moody often helped to ease their collective burdens by purchasing these items and distributing them.

On one memorable occasion, Moody even played amateur detective and foiled an attempt to steal a large cache of coal he had obtained for the use of poor families. An account in the *Chicago Tribune* stated: "Two men [have been] arrested on a complaint of [D. L.] Moody who . . . discovered that they have been fraudulently delivering coal which had been secured for poor relief. It appears that Mr. Moody, having a donation of several hundred tons of coal, hired the Fishers to transport the same from the Rock Island freight depot to the society's [City

Relief Society] yard. Moody apparently acted as his own detective and made the complaint himself."[33]

~

Once Moody had been able to add a new boy or girl to his quickly growing class, he took steps to keep them there. His son, Will, recalled the following:

> ... among the premiums for good conduct and regular attendance, one summer season, thirteen boys were promised a new suit each at Christmas if they would attend regularly until that time. [These were] their descriptive names ... Red Eye, Smikes, Madden the Butcher, Jackey Candles, Giberick, Billy Blucannon, Darby the Cobbler, Butcher Lilray, Greenhorn, Indian, Black Stove Pipe, Old Man, and Rag-Breeches Cadet.
>
> All but one fulfilled the conditions, and [Father] had them photographed "before" and "after" the donning of the suits, the pictures entitled, "Does it Pay?" and "It Does Pay!" This uniformed group became known as "Moody's bodyguard."[34]

Dickens's Ebenezer Scrooge had no change of heart until he was an elderly man—nor did the poor of his fictional London know kindness or generosity from his hand, save for the last few years of his life. One has only to look at the picture Moody had commissioned of him and his bodyguard to know how thoroughly Dickens's fictional paradigm had been turned on its head. Moody was scarcely older than his boys, but he had given himself completely in service to them.

That old photograph is a moment in real time: an image of destitute lives transformed. Moody's Sunday school would go on to larger buildings and even host a visit from Abraham Lincoln. But it would never know a more glorious moment than this.

4

THE COMING OF WAR

In 1857 there was a revival that swept over this country—some people took up the pen and tried to write it down; it swept over the east and on to the western cities, clear over to the Pacific coast. This was God calling the nation to himself. There were half a million people united with the church at that time. Then the war broke out. We were baptized with the Holy Ghost in 1857, and in 1861 we were baptized in blood.[1]

—D. L. Moody

When President-Elect Abraham Lincoln visited D. L. Moody's Sunday school in November 1860, it was more than a time when the man soon to be inaugurated as America's sixteenth president spoke poignantly. It was an event rich in symbolism, a harbinger of events that would change America forever.

For a brief moment, Lincoln had been given the happy task of speaking to children whose lives were being transformed for the better through the ministry Moody and his coworkers had launched in the slums of Chicago. But what neither he nor Moody knew was how quickly the dread specter of civil war would overtake them—and, indeed, so many of the young people Lincoln had addressed. When the Civil War commenced in 1861, approximately seventy-five of the boys to whom Lincoln had spoken would take up arms to defend the Union. Some would give their lives for it.

～

The Civil War was a crucible for D. L. Moody, but not in the way one might expect. For reasons of conscience, he did not enlist in the Union army, but along with John Farwell and another Chicago friend, B. F. Jacobs, he organized an army and navy committee of the Chicago YMCA, which later became a branch of the United States Christian Commission.[2]

But he was not solely an organizer. He actively took part as a volunteer in the Commission's mission of promoting "the spiritual good, intellectual improvement, and social and physical comfort"[3] of the soldiers. On nine occasions he traveled to the front with the Union army during the war.[4]

At the outset of hostilities, however, Moody's work as a relief worker centered on Camp Douglas, a military outpost designed to facilitate the training of citizen soldiers from all over the northwest. The camp was located just a few miles south of Chicago, and in the words of John Farwell, it became Moody's "kindergarten of training."[5]

Moody's role developed over time into a position that was one part chaplain-at-large, one part relief worker. It was an ad hoc arrangement to be sure, but one that drew on his gifts for organization and fostered his burgeoning gifts as a preacher.

It was also a role that taxed even his prodigious physical reserves to the limit. He was going from sunup to sundown, and far on into the night—every night. "I have some 500 or 800 people that are dependent on me for their daily food & new ones [are] coming all the time," he wrote to his brother Samuel in January 1862.

> I keep a sadall horse to ride around with to hunt up the poore people with & then I keep a nother horse & man to carry around the things with & then I have a man to waite on the folks as they come to my office. I make my headquarters at the roomes of the Young Mens Christian Association & then I have just raised money enough to erect a chapel for the soldiers at camp 3 miles from the city so you see I have 3 meetigs to atend to every day be side calling on the sick and that is not all. I have to go into the countrey about every week to buy wood and provisions for the poor also coal wheet meal and corn.[6]

≈

What lingered long after Moody's wartime service were the scenes and people he encountered. They became the subject of stories he told time and again from the pulpit—for they had taught him things he never forgot, and wished to tell others.

Moody had many gifts as a storyteller and was equally adept at mingling humor and pathos or illustrating spiritual truths through his personal experiences. The following story, concerning the Battle of Pittsburg Landing—or, as it is better known, the Battle of Shiloh—is taken from a stenographer's transcript of one of Moody's later sermons.

On the morning of April 6, 1862, Confederate forces commanded by Albert Sidney Johnston attacked General Ulysses S. Grant's encampment near Pittsburg Landing, beginning the bloodiest engagement of the war.[7] The fighting lasted for two days, resulting in a narrow victory for Union forces; but one secured at a horrific cost. Shiloh was a battle in which more than 13,047 Union soldiers had been killed—nearly 24,000 thousand men in all when Confederate casualties (10,699) were taken into account.[8] Moody was with Grant and an eyewitness to it all—the carnage, the desperate heroism, and heart-rending visits to offer what comfort could be given to the dying. It's little wonder that he never forgot what he saw, or that these memories would have figured so prominently in sermons he later gave.

It was a deathbed scene that Moody later recounted in a sermon:

> I don't care how far down you have gone nor how deep the pit into which you have fallen, [God] can lift you up and transform you, as we know from the third chapter of John. I want

to tell you how I read that chapter one night, when it sounded sweeter than ever it did before. I was [with] the army of General Grant. After the terrible battle of Pittsburgh Landing [in April 1862,] I was in a hospital at Murfreesboro looking after the wounded and dying. I had been up two nights and was so utterly exhausted that I almost went to sleep while walking around among the cots of the wounded soldiers, and I was obliged to take a little rest. Just as I had fallen asleep in the middle of the night a soldier woke me up and said that a man in a certain ward wanted to see me.

"Well," I said, "I will see him in the morning."

"But," he said, "he will be dead in the morning; if you want to see him you must come now."

So I went with him, and he led me to the wounded man's cot. The dying soldier said: "Chaplain, I want you to help me die."

"My dear friend," I said, "I would take you right up in my arms and carry you into the kingdom of God if I could; but I cannot do it; I cannot help you die."

"But, Chaplain, can't you help me see the way; it is hard to die all alone."

I tell you that is when we want help. I told him about Jesus Christ; but he shook his head and said: "He won't help me, because I have been fighting against Him all my life."

He said that when he told his mother he had enlisted she said: "I could give you up and let you go if you were only a Christian; but the thought that you may be cut down and die without Christ is terrible to me."

"I told mother that when the war was over I would become a Christian. 'But,' said she, 'You may never live to see this war over'; and now I have got to die, and I never shall see her again. Can't you help me?"

"I will do all I can," I said.

I took my Bible and read the promises to him, but I couldn't get him to believe that one of those promises was for him. I saw that his life was fast slipping away, and I couldn't bear to have him die in that condition; so I lifted my heart to God for direction. Then I turned to the third chapter of John, and said: "I am going to read a conversation that Christ had with a man who went to Him in your state of mind."

So I began: "There was a man of the Pharisees, named Nicodemus, a ruler of the Jews: The same came to Jesus by night, and said unto him, Rabbi, we know that thou art a teacher come from God: for no man can do these miracles that thou doest, except God be with him."

The dying man's eyes were riveted upon me, as he eagerly listened to every word that fell from my lips, and when I got to the fourteenth verse and read, "And as Moses lifted up the serpent in the wilderness, even so must the Son of man be lifted up: That whosoever believeth in Him should not perish, but have eternal life," he cried:

"Stop, is that there?"

"Yes," I said, "it is right here."

"Read that again, will you?"

I read it slowly and carefully that he might hear every word: "As Moses lifted up the serpent in the wilderness, even so must the Son of man be lifted up: That whosoever believeth in Him should not perish, but have eternal life."

Then he said: "That helps."

"Well," I said, "bless God for that!"

"It sounds good, Chaplain, read it to me once more," he said.

And I read it again. A radiant smile came over his face, and it seemed as if a new life had dawned upon him. When I had finished the chapter, I sat quietly beside him for some time. I noticed that his lips were moving, and I thought perhaps he was trying to pray. I bent over him and I could hear him faintly whisper, "That whosoever believeth in Him should not perish, but have eternal life."

Then he opened his eyes, fixed a calm, resigned look upon me and said: "Chaplain, you needn't read to me any more; it is enough; Jesus Christ was lifted up in my place. I am not alone now."

After I had prayed with him and made him as comfortable as possible, I left him for the night. The next morning I hastened back to the ward. The cot was empty. I asked the nurse: "Did you stay with him till he died?"

"Yes."

"Tell me how he died?"

"Why," said she, "he kept repeating those verses over and over again, and just as he breathed his last I heard him say, 'As Moses lifted up the serpent in the wilderness, even so must the Son of man be lifted up!'"

I thank God for the third chapter of John! I think it is the most precious thing in all the world.[9]

~

C. F. Goss, who had hired the stenographer to take down the Moody sermon in which this story appeared, summarized Moody's wartime service as well as anyone ever did. Speaking of these years, he concluded: "The effect of this terrible experience upon [Mr. Moody's] mind can be traced through all the rest of his life in many of his sermons and addresses. The immense activities which he beheld, the mighty organization of the army, the heroism of the men in battle, their patience in suffering, their gratitude for kindness . . . their spiritual natures in sickness and death . . . the blood, the tears, the carnage . . . lent a new color, deep, somber, [and] solemn—to all he did and said."[10]

Goss could not have been more just in what he said. Years after the war's close, Moody observed in a sermon:

In this country our forefathers planted slavery in the face of an open Bible, and didn't we have to reap? When the harvest came, nearly half a million of our young men were buried, many of them in nameless graves. Didn't God make this nation weep in the hour of gathering the harvest, when we had to give up our young men, both North and South, to death; and almost every household had an empty chair, and blood, blood, blood, flowed like water for four long years? Ah, our nation sowed, and how in tears and groans she had to reap![11]

EMMA

All is holy where devotion kneels.[1]

—Oliver Wendell Holmes

But not all was devastation for D. L. Moody during the Civil War. He married Emma Charlotte Revell on Thursday, August 28, 1862. No man ever received a finer wife as a gift from the Lord.

Nevertheless, the challenge Emma Moody faced as a wife was little different from that confronting Alice Lee when she married Theodore Roosevelt in 1880. For in terms of energy and the sheer force of his personality, D. L. Moody was every inch the counterpart of the man known to history as "T. Vesuvius Roosevelt."[2]

Right from the start, Emma Moody knew that hers would not be a conventional marriage. But though her personality differed greatly from her husband's—she was cultured, demure, and without his seemingly boundless physical energy—she

49

was a force to be reckoned with in her own right. She may have had delicate features and was sometimes physically frail, but there was something about her spirit—and there always would be—that was undaunted. Once, during a trip to England (the Moodys had taken a sea voyage as a means of therapeutic treatment for Emma's asthma), she had to make a brief trip alone by train. Stepping aboard, she made her way to what she thought was an empty compartment, save for a bundle of old clothes. Then, as J. C. Pollock wrote:

> The train started. Out of the bundle a man's voice said, "Do you know what I would have done with my wives if I had been Henry the Eighth?" He slid across to her side, leering. No trains had corridors in the 1860s. The next stop lay twenty minutes on.
>
> Emma, unrattled always, merely said, "No, do tell me." The maniac recited blood-curdling details, with strong hints that he intended to test his theories on her. When he paused to enjoy the effect of his words, she briskly said she knew better ways of execution, and each time he suggested a horror she capped it, keeping him still and absorbed until the train stopped and she escaped.[3]

≈

Emma Moody's pluck, composure, and gentle courage were complemented by another trait: she was also a young woman of keen insight, who readily discerned the sterling qualities in the man she had chosen to wed. And she knew they shared a deep, abiding faith—as well as a heart for service and ministry.

They had first gotten to know one another in Chicago in 1858 when Moody noticed her as a fifteen-year-old new teacher for girls in a Sunday school he sometimes attended on Wells Street.[4] He soon began calling at the Washington Street home where Emma and her English émigré family lived.

With a circle of young men in tow—there were three marriageable Revell sisters—Moody would come to call on Emma. The entire company, young men and women, would cluster close by a sheet-iron stove on winter nights and form a merry gathering. Emma's little nine-year-old brother Fleming sometimes hid himself within earshot and caught snatches of their conversation.[5]

Moody was bowled over by this pretty girl with her "quiet maturity and happy laugh."[6] And if he was like Teddy Roosevelt in energy and force of personality, his resolve to win her was no less ardent than TR's resolve to win the unattainable Alice Lee had been during his undergraduate years at Harvard. Bumptious and awkward Moody may have been, as TR then was. And unlike TR, he could also at times be crude and uncouth in his ways. But he had set his cap for Emma Revell, and would do whatever it took to win her. Still, he would have to bide his time. No thought of engagement could be entertained until she turned seventeen—two years hence.[7] Even then, he would have to wait two more years before they could marry.

Emma, it seems, was drawn rather quickly to this overgrown and unkempt puppy of a young man. Perhaps it was something about his vitality that initially appealed to her, suffering as she did from episodes of asthma and recurrent headaches. But then, there were also reserves of tenderness and great kindness that flowed into Moody's work among the children of Little Hell. She knew that. She also knew how selflessly he gave himself to them. There were the raw materials of a very good man here, though sometimes obscured beneath a rough-hewn exterior.[8] Emma saw them for what they were.

Straightaway, it seems, she began to smooth his rough edges. She was only fifteen, and he a very independent-minded young man of twenty, but he assented. He was too deeply in love to kick at the traces over much. Their son Paul described his father's high regard and love for his mother: "My father's admiration for [my mother] was as boundless as his love. To the day of his death, I believe, he never ceased to wonder at two things—the use God had made of him despite his handicaps, and the miracle of having won the love of a woman he considered so completely his superior."[9]

~

Following a brief honeymoon, the Moodys took up residence in a tiny house in the then slummy north side of Chicago.[10] Emma's pluck and gentle courage may have been more understated than her husband's, but they were no less strong than the faith-based devotion each bore for the untouchables of that great city. They would serve God and those children together.

They were deeply in love, but that did not mean there wasn't a fair share of the comic at times. Where she was "practical and orderly,"[11] his habits often ran in the other direction.

He was fond of wearing patent shirts because, among other things, he claimed they did not need washing for weeks. She threw them away. She was less successful at getting him to eat regular meals, but she would bide her time.[12] He wanted to do as well by her as she did by him. They would go on together.

And they grew together—over a marriage of almost forty years. Near the end of that time, they had become so close and so united in purpose that Moody could say: "She was the only one who never tried to hold me back from anything I wanted to do, and was always in sympathy with every new venture."[13] They were by this time more alike than anyone save themselves knew.

6

"A DIFFERENT GOSPEL"

Nothing but what astonishes is true.[1]

—Edward Young

D. L. Moody had great power before, but nothing like
what he had after dear Harry Morehouse came into our
lives.[2]

—Fleming H. Revell

Moody told a story of how he had been not only
wrong but spectacularly wrong. His coming to
terms with that fact changed the course of his life
and ministry. Had this transformation not taken place, he would
never have become the herald of God's grace, mercy, and love
so many remembered him to be.

That Moody told this account publicly says something
about him. The story of his change of heart was intended to

be an object lesson, the point of which was "don't fall into the same trap I once did." It was an unflinching *mea culpa*.

He told a large audience one memorable evening: "There was a time when I preached that God hated the sinner, and that God was after every poor sinner with a double-edged sword."[3] He may well have paused to let that thought sink in.

He then continued,

But I have changed my ideas upon this point. I will tell you how.[4]

In 1867, when I was preaching in Dublin, in a large hall, at the close of the service, a young man who did not look over seventeen, though he was older, came up to me and said he would like to go back to America with me and preach the gospel.[5]

I measured him all over, and he repeated his request, and asked me when I was going back. I told him I didn't know; probably I should not have told him if I had known.[6]

He asked me if I would write to him when I went, and he would come with me. When I went I thought I would not write to him, as I did not know whether I wanted him or not.

After I arrived at Chicago, I got a letter saying he had just arrived at New York, and he would come and preach. I wrote him a cold letter, [grudgingly saying he might] call on me if he came west.

A few days after, I got a letter stating he would be in Chicago next Thursday. I didn't know what to do with him. I said to the officers of the church: "There is a man coming from England, and he wants to preach. I am going to be absent on Thursday and Friday. If you will let him preach on those days, I will be back on Saturday, and take him off your hands."

[And so,] at my request, they let him preach. On my return on Saturday I was anxious to hear how the people liked him, and I asked my wife how that young Englishman got along.

"How did they like him?"

She said, "They liked him very much. *He preaches a little different from what you do. He tells people God loves them.* I think you will like him."

I said he was wrong. I thought I could not like a man who preached contrary to what I was preaching. I went down Saturday night to hear him, but I had made up my mind not to like him because he preached different from me.

[That evening] he took his text . . . the third chapter of John and the sixteenth verse . . . He preached a wonderful sermon from that text. "For God so loved the world that he gave his only begotten Son, that whosoever believeth in him should not perish, but have everlasting life."

My wife had told me he had preached the two previous sermons from that text, and I noticed there was a smile over the house when he took the same text. Instead of preaching that God was behind them with a double-edged sword to hew them down, he told them God wanted every sinner to be saved, and He loved them.

I could not keep back the tears. I didn't know God

thought so much of me. It was wonderful to hear the way he brought out Scripture. He went from Genesis to Revelation, and preached that in all ages, God loved the sinner.

On Sunday night, there was a great crowd came to hear him. He took for his text the third chapter of John and sixteenth verse, and he preached his fourth sermon from that wonderful text, "For God so loved the world," &c., and he went from Genesis to Revelation to show that it was love, love, love, that brought Christ from Heaven, that made him step from the throne to lift up this poor, fallen world. He struck a higher chord that night, and it was glorious.

The next night there was an immense crowd, and he said: "Turn to the third chapter and 16th verse of John," and he preached his fifth sermon from that wonderful text. He did not divide the text up into firstly, secondly, and thirdly, but he took the whole text and threw it at them. I thought that sermon was better than ever. I got so full of love that I got up and told my friends how much God loved them.

The whole church was on fire before the week was over. Tuesday night came, and there was a greater crowd than ever. The preacher said: "Turn to the third chapter of John and the 16th verse and you will find my text," and he preached his sixth sermon from that wonderful text . . . They thought that sermon was better than any of the rest. It seemed as if every heart was on fire, and sinners came pressing into the kingdom of God.

On Wednesday night people thought that probably he would change his text now, as he could not talk any longer on love. There was great excitement to see what he was going to say. He stood before us again and he said: "My friends, I have been trying to get a new text, but I cannot find any as good as the old one, so we will again turn to the third chapter of John and the 16th verse."

He preached his seventh sermon from that wonderful text.

I have never forgotten those nights. I have preached a different gospel since, and I have had more power with God and man since . . . In closing up that seventh sermon he said: "For seven nights I have been trying to tell you how much God loved you, but this poor stammering tongue of mine will not let me. If I could ascend Jacob's ladder and ask Gabriel, who stands in the presence of the Almighty, to tell me how much love God the father has for this poor lost world, all that Gabriel could say would be 'That God so loved the world that he gave his only begotten Son, that whosoever believeth in him should not perish but have everlasting life.'"[7]

Henry "Harry" Morehouse, born in Lancashire, England, in 1850, had an early life even more peripatetic than Moody's had been. Few would have marked him out as a preacher, let alone one who could speak with such power. Before he was twenty-one, he had served time in prison. A petty thief, adept at picking pockets, he was converted when he discovered a back-street mission where a former boxer and coal miner were taking it in turns to preach on the parable of the prodigal son. Slowly, fitfully, he was transformed—though he had to wear thick gloves for a time to avoid lapsing into his pickpocket ways.[8]

By the time he was twenty-seven, Harry Morehouse's life was radically different. He had become a reputable auctioneer and married a childhood sweetheart. Not long after, he purchased a small cottage just outside the great city of Manchester and made the decision to give his life fully to preaching.[9] Coming under the influence of the Plymouth Brethren, Morehouse became a keen student of Scripture. His studies lent a richness to his preaching that belied his lack of formal training.[10]

If Moody could have brought himself to admit it earlier, he and Harry Morehouse were much alike. Both had a keen sense of humor verging on the whimsical or ludicrous, a capacity for gentleness and self-effacing humility, and "an ability to prick any bubble of pretension or cant."[11]

It was strange providence, but nonetheless true: Moody's entire approach to proclaiming the gospel was redirected through the influence of a former convict. He hadn't seen it coming but could rejoice afterward in the truth that "a gracious hand leads us in ways we know not."[12]

Moody sheathed the double-edged sword he had formerly wielded in the name of the Lord and unfurled a banner of love. Family and friends immediately noticed the great change. One friend, John Milton Hitchcock, wrote that it was during this time that he heard Moody preach "the most impassioned, powerful, incisive, pathetic and effective appeals I ever knew him to make."[13]

There is a sequel to Harry Morehouse's first visit to Chicago. "I have preached a different gospel since," Moody said, and I have had more power with God and man since then. In closing up that seventh sermon he said: "For seven nights I have been trying to tell you how much God loved you, but this poor stammering tongue of mine will not let me. If I could ascend Jacob's ladder and ask Gabriel, who stands in the presence of the Almighty, to tell me how much love God the father has for this poor lost world, all that Gabriel could say would be, 'God so loved the world, that He gave His only begotten Son, that whosoever believeth in Him should not perish, but have everlasting life.'" He went to Europe and returned again. In the meantime our church had been burned, and a temporary building had been erected. When he returned he preached in this building, and said: "Although the old building is burnt up, the old text is not burnt up, and we will preach from that." So he preached from where he had left off before, about the love of God.[14]

≈

Love, as expressed in John 3:16, now became the hallmark of Moody's preaching. Grace and mercy were its attendants. "Love is the lever," he declared, "with which Christ lifts the world."[15]

Moody held to this truth with an ardor that only increased with time. That this was true was captured in a story he told nearly twenty years after he met Harry Morehouse:

I was staying with a party of friends in a country house during my visit to England in 1884. On Sunday evening as we sat around the fire, they asked me to read and expound some portion of Scripture. Being tired after the services of the day, I told them to ask Henry Drummond, who was one of the party. After some urging, he drew a small [New] Testament from his hip pocket, opened it at the 13th chapter of First Corinthians, and began to speak on the subject of Love.

It seemed to me that I had never heard anything so beautiful, and I determined not to rest until I brought Henry Drummond to Northfield to deliver that address. Since then I have requested the principals of my schools to have it read before the students every year. The one great need in our Christian life is love, more love to God and to each other. Would that we could all move into that Love chapter, and live there.[16]

7

BRANDS FROM THE BURNING

Late in the evening of [Sunday] the eighth [of October 1871] the fire had started in DeKoven Street . . . Aided by a strong southwest wind it swept away the wooden structures in the neighborhood and was soon beyond control.

Then, for two nights and two days, it mowed its awful way through the greatest city of the West, leaving behind it a scene of smoldering ruin such as has seldom been witnessed . . .

Almost one hundred thousand were driven from their homes. Over 17,000 buildings were destroyed, including all of those in the business section. On seventy-three miles of streets not a single habitation was left standing.[1]

—*The Burning of Chicago: Poems of the Great Chicago Fire*

When the city bell first rang the alarm for what would come to be known as the "Great Chicago Fire," D. L. Moody was in the midst of preaching a sermon in the second Farwell Hall, the YMCA building he and so many others cherished, since the first Farwell Hall had been lost to fire within four months of its dedication in 1867.[2]

Like most who heard him that night, Moody thought nothing of the alarm at first. He, like them, had become somewhat inured to the sound, for fires—always tragic events to be sure—were commonplace in 1870s America.[3] Hopefully, this fire could be quickly contained.

But it wasn't. As Moody's service drew to a close, the bell began to ring out a general alarm. Many people quickly departed following the last hymn, but the general sense of unease was not yet pervasive enough to dissuade Moody from holding an inquiry meeting for any who wished to talk with him or his ministry coworkers further about the truth-claims of Christianity.[4] In the event, the meeting proved to be of short duration, for in his sermon he had asked his audience to go home and ponder the question, "What shall I do with Jesus, who is called Christ?" and to return the following Sunday, when he would unfold the answer that had transformed his life—and he hoped, would transform theirs. People were not to be blamed for taking him at this word and simply going home to think over what he had said.

Almost immediately after Moody exited Farwell Hall, an apocalyptic scene met his eyes. Off in the distance, fire was breaking out all around.

He was then met by a searing hurricane-force wind, which caught up burning debris from buildings already ablaze and set others alight. As he rushed home and entered the door of his home, all he could think to say to Emma was, "The city's doomed."

By midnight, much of Chicago was caught up in a horrific bedlam: Buildings fell in upon themselves. Terrified people and horses screamed amidst the roar of the flames. The streets were thronged with firefighters trying to do what they could, as well as an ever-increasing crowd of refugees.

Bravely, perhaps foolishly, Moody's stalwart friend Ira Sankey made his way back to Farwell Hall and retrieved a few precious belongings before the building was lost. He then rushed to the shore of Lake Michigan, where many others had sought refuge.[5]

Meanwhile, Moody saw no immediate need to flee his home on State Street. The flames were as yet somewhat distant from the district in which he lived. Then, in the early morning hours, a policeman's knock at the door roused the entire household. "We're telling people to leave," he said.

Hastily, the Moodys began to gather what little belongings they could carry. Just outside their door, looting had begun— bringing yet another threat of violence. Moody quickly arranged for a nearby neighbor who owned a horse and buggy to take his children and the neighbor's own to a place of safety in a northern suburb. This seen to, he placed the few belongings he wished to save into a pram and made ready to leave.

But Emma caught his arm, pleading with him to take the portrait that artist G. P. A. Healy had only recently painted of him. Moody thought the idea ludicrous. "Take my own picture!"

he said, laughing. "That would be a joke. Suppose I meet some friends in the same trouble as ourselves and they say, 'Hullo Moody, glad you have escaped. What's that you've saved and cling to so affectionately.' Wouldn't it sound well to reply, 'Oh, I've got my own portrait!'"

He had scarcely finished saying this than looters burst through the door. At times the surreal experience of a fire can produce strange things. Such was the case now. Not one looter threatened the Moodys. In fact, when one of them heard them disputing about the Healy portrait, he showed a bizarre form of gallantry, cut it from its frame, and handed it to Emma. She took it, and they quickly left.

As they rushed to the home of Emma's sister, Sarah Holden, in a safe western suburb, Moody heard a voice, crying, "Mr. Moody, please save my doll!" He looked and saw a little girl paralyzed by fright in the door or window of a nearby house. He dashed to the house and carried the child to safety. He and Emma then made for her sister's home.[6] When they arrived, he could take some solace in knowing his family was safe. He knew little else besides.

~

Moody's recollections of this disaster would forever remain vivid. "Before midnight," he said:

> [Farwell Hall] was in ashes; before two o'clock the [Illinois Street] church where I worshiped was in ashes; before three o'clock the house that I lived in was in ashes.

Before daybreak next morning, one hundred thousand people were burned out of house and home. It seemed to me that I had a glimpse in that fire of what the Day of Judgment will be, when I saw flames rolling down the streets, twenty and thirty feet high, consuming everything in its march that did not flee. I saw there the millionaire and the beggar fleeing alike. There was no difference. That night great men, learned men, wise men, all fled.[7]

Moody had seen "people rush through the streets crazed with fear" and he would learn something that filled him with an abiding grief. "Some of those," he said, "who were at the [Farwell Hall] meeting were burned to death."[8]

Years later, when preaching at the Chicago World's Fair, the memory of that tragedy still haunted him:

I have never seen that [Farwell Hall] congregation since. I have hard work to keep back the tears to-day. I have looked over this audience, and not a single one is here that I preached to that night. I have a great many old friends and am pretty well acquainted in Chicago, but twenty-two years have passed away, and I have not seen that congregation since, and I never will meet those people again until I meet them in another world.

But I want to tell you of one lesson I learned that night, which I have never forgotten, and that is, when I preach, to press Christ upon the people then and there, and try to bring them to a decision on the spot. I would rather have that right hand cut off than to give an audience now a week to decide what to do with Jesus. [For this,] I have often been criticized; people have said:

"Moody, you seem to be trying to get people to decide all at once: why do you not give them time to consider?" [In reply, I tell them of the Chicago Fire.]

I have asked God many times to forgive me for telling people that night to take a week to think it over . . . I will never do it again.[9]

~

In the aftermath of the Chicago fire, Moody traveled east to raise funds to rebuild the Illinois Street Church and underwrite the cost of a new temporary structure in which services could be held, to be called the North Side Tabernacle.

God granted him good success, as he related in the following story:

After the big Chicago fire I came to New York for money, and I heard there was a rich man in Fall River [Massachusetts] who was very [generous]. So I went to him. He gave me a check for a large amount, and then got into his carriage and drove with me to the houses of other rich men in the city, and they all gave me checks. When he left me at the train I grasped his hand and said:

"If you ever come to Chicago, call on me, and I will return your favor."

He said: "Mr. Moody, don't wait for me; do it to the first man that comes along."

I never forget that remark; it had the ring of the true
good Samaritan.[10]

Along with sending the proceeds back, he telegraphed
his friends to "build large"—a motto, his friend Charles Goss
observed, "that might be chosen by him as the best expression
of his life purpose."[11]

Moody's use of the phrase "build large" was indica-
tive of the man, but in another very telling way it could have
been a reflection of Moody's putting on a brave face. For as
Goss observed, it was during this period back east that Moody
"passed through the only recorded period of profound spiritual
disturbance in his whole life." "It seemed," he said, "as if the
Lord was taking him to pieces."[12]

Unbeknownst to anyone, save perhaps Emma, Moody had
for nearly four months been in the midst of an agonizing and
intense spiritual crisis, or what has often been called "a dark
night of the soul."[13] Aside from the recent devastation of the
Chicago Fire, a contributing factor may have been the stress
of overwork, because the pace he set—with meetings, organiz-
ing, and the like—often left hale and hearty men straining to
keep up. It may also have been that like his younger contemporary, Theodore Roosevelt, Moody had for many years been
laboring unconsciously under a burden best described in TR's
phrase: "Black care rarely sits behind a rider whose pace is fast
enough."[14]

For all the rough edges that showed themselves at times in
his habits and character, and despite the tremendous physical

energy and reserves he so often drew upon, Moody was also a man who throughout his life demonstrated a great tenderness and sensitivity.[15] He was a man of hidden depths. His description of his feelings immediately after his conversion is but one instance of this. There was something of the rough-hewn poet in him, and here one thinks of a spiritual forbear like John Newton—a man in whom there were poetic lines of the *Olney Hymns*, as well as a roughness of character stemming from many stormy experiences of life.

Newton had times of spiritual crisis, resulting in a deepening faith and a more profound sense of the Holy Spirit's work in his life. Moody was now similarly circumstanced. "God seemed to be showing me myself," he wrote. "I found everything in my heart that ought not to be there. For four months a wrestling went on in me. I was a miserable man."[16]

Moody believed a consuming ambition was at the root of his trouble. "I found I was ambitious," he said. "I was not preaching for Christ; I was preaching for ambition." It was as much as saying, "Maybe the shoe salesman bent on amassing a fortune of $100,000 is not as far removed from who I am now as I thought." Such searching questions, when honestly confronted for the first time, can lead to a questioning of one's identity and life purpose. This seems to be just what Moody was contending with.

The final resolution of Moody's spiritual conflict was something he seldom referred to, as he considered it "almost too sacred an experience to name."[17] But one day in late autumn, as he walked the streets of New York City, "crying all the time that God would fill me with his Spirit . . . God revealed himself to me, and I had such an experience of his love that I had to ask him to stay his hand."[18]

Speaking about this on another occasion, he said:

> I had returned to God again, and I was wretched no longer . . . [God] filled me so full of the Spirit. If I have not been a different man since, I do not know myself . . . But O it was preceded by a wrestling and hard struggle! [I could only think of my] miserable selfishness [and how] I wanted to see my little vineyard blessed . . . But I could work for the whole world now. I would like to go round the world and tell the perishing millions of a Saviour's love.[19]

Moody's time of spiritual conflict and resolution left him forever changed. Just how that change would work itself out in his life remained to be seen. But what he knew now, and what mattered most, was that he had come to a place of blessing unlike anything he had ever known. It was a place of peace.

8

WHAT HAPPENED
AT YORK

I have no doubt that if I had known when I reached
England of what was before me I would have been
frightened.[1]

—D. L. Moody, 1875

The greatest preaching tour Moody ever undertook
nearly came to grief before it had begun. In June 1873,
at the invitation of friends in Britain, he took ship with
Ira Sankey for what would be his third visit to that country. Both
cherished the hope of conducting an extensive series of evangelistic meetings throughout the British Isles.

He had no way of knowing that he would arrive nearly
penniless and at the risk of his life. All he knew was that he was
filled with the desire "to dream great things for God. To get
back to Great Britain and win ten thousand souls."[2]

But first he had to bid farewell to Chicago—a difficult and bittersweet task. In ways that perhaps he only half understood, Moody felt that in the aftermath of the Great Chicago Fire, it was time to leave the city that had become his second home. The invitations he had received to preach in Britain had stirred something deep within him and, as John Pollock noted, "his heart was across the sea."[3] Throughout the winter of 1872–1873, he gave clear indications to John Farwell and his other friends in Chicago that he would be leaving.

Farwell tried to dissuade him. "I did all I could to persuade him to stay and help build up from the ruins of the fire along religious lines, but to no effect."[4] Still, although his intention to leave was unchanged, Moody did what he could to set the ministry in Chicago on a footing whereby it could begin anew. Ever devoted to the YMCA, he took a leading role in raising funds for a third Farwell Hall. He also launched an appeal for funds to build a permanent replacement for the Tabernacle that had served as a temporary home for the Illinois Street Church since the Great Fire. This resulted in the purchase of a site at the corner of La Salle Street and Chicago Avenue—the future home of what would eventually become the Moody Memorial Church. Once builders had set to work on this permanent church home, he knew it was time to leave.

Farwell, sadly reconciled to Moody's departure, proved a faithful friend. His parting gift was as gallant as it was generous—a check for five hundred dollars. If his friend had to leave, he would do what he could to see him well on his way. In reply, Moody wrote a heartfelt letter on June 7, part of which read:

I want to thank you for the $500. I can't tell you how much I
appreciate it, and all your acts of love and kindness. It is a
wonder to me at times, and I do not see why you do not get
sick of me and cast me off. The more I know of myself, the
less I think of myself.

> Good bye, from your old friend,
> D. L. Moody[5]

Farwell's parting gift had indeed been generous, but
Moody had scarcely received it when money matters of a different and near catastrophic nature reared their head without
warning.

These concerns were as yet unknown when the Moodys
and Sankeys arrived in Liverpool, England, on June 17, 1873.
Only when they disembarked did they learn of the deaths of
three men—William Pennefather, Henry Bewley, and Cuthbert
Bainbridge—who had pledged to pay the expenses of their
evangelistic tour.[6]

Dumbstruck and dismayed, the Moodys and Sankeys parted
to find temporary lodgings. Moody and his wife, Emma, traveled to stay with her family in London, while Ira Sankey and his
wife, Fanny, went to stay with Henry Morehouse and his family in the city of Manchester. All they knew to do was to pray.
They did not know what else could be done.[7]

A glimmer of hope emerged a short time later when
Moody remembered an invitation he had received from George
Bennett, a chemist in the great Cathedral city of York who was
a leading organizer of that city's YMCA. Moody sent word to

Sankey: "Here is a door which is partly open, and we will go there and begin our work."[8]

This seemed well enough, but what Moody had forgotten—even as he remembered Bennett's invitation—was that he had never responded one way or the other to that invitation. The first word of any kind Bennett received was relayed by telegram on June 18. Sent by a friend at the YMCA in Liverpool, it came as a bolt from the blue: "MOODY HERE. ARE YOU READY FOR HIM?"[9] Caught completely unaware, Bennett took two days to reply. His telegram seemed intended to give himself a little time to prepare for Moody's arrival: "PLEASE FIX DATE WHEN YOU CAN COME TO YORK."[10]

Moody, who at age thirty-six was still very much given to acting on impulse, decided to head to York by himself to investigate the possibilities. Sankey, for a time, would remain behind. He wired Bennett immediately: "I WILL BE IN YORK TONIGHT TEN O'CLOCK. STOP. MAKE NO ARRANGEMENTS TILL I COME."[11]

When Bennett and Moody met in York on Friday, June 20, at the train station, Moody was all action. "How far is it to Manchester?" he asked. "I might have meetings there first before York."[12]

Bennett was clearly still a bit shell-shocked. "It's sixty or seventy miles," he replied. "You can't go now. Come with me for supper, and stay the night anyhow. Then we can talk it over."[13]

Moody agreed, and the two walked together to Bennett's chemist shop on New Bridge Street. As they dined, Moody stated his intentions with all the directness of the businessman he had once been in Chicago—a businessman alive to opportunities—opportunities he now wished to pursue with a holy boldness. It was as he later explained: "I am a man of impulse. The best things I have ever done have been decided on the impulse."[14]

And so he told Bennett: "Every man has to make his own way, so I propose we make arrangements tomorrow, Saturday, to commence meetings Sunday. You telegraph [Henry] Moorhouse to have Sankey here sometime tomorrow."[15]

When Moody had arrived in York, "no one except his friend [George] Bennett had ever seen him, and very few had ever heard his name."[16] This seemed a prime reason why the first Sunday morning meeting that was held proved inauspicious and unpromising at best. Instead of looking out over a sea of curious faces, Moody looked out over a small stream at best of what seemed to be dour, unresponsive faces. An afternoon meeting was planned for the Corn Exchange, a large, ugly building that seemed ill-suited for anything like a religious gathering. As he exited the Sunday morning meeting, Moody could have been forgiven for yielding to crestfallen hopes, but he seemed ebullient—almost as though he knew something was in the wind. On his way over to the Corn Exchange, Moody stopped and gathered up a small cache of Bibles. He turned to Ira Sankey and said, "Now, Sankey, you bring a pile of Bibles."

At this, George Bennett said, "What do you want to do?"

Moody's reply must have been slightly unnerving. "Oh," he said, "I shall have your hair standing straight on your head before I have finished in York!"[17]

When the three men arrived at the Corn Exchange, an audience of eight hundred awaited them. It was somewhat less than the venue could hold, but it was a good-sized crowd. Moody must have cut an eccentric figure as he entered, toting more than a few Bibles that seemed to have sprouted white slips of paper, upon which were written a number and a verse of Scripture. With him was Sankey, holding more or less the same number of Bibles with protruding slips of paper.[18]

Moving briskly, Moody waded into the crowd and began handing out Bibles at random. "Read the text when I call your number!" he said heartily to each person he gave one to. Once he had finished, he started the meeting.[19]

It was Moody at his unconventional best. As the *Yorkshire Gazette* reported, it was a "somewhat novel but very profitable Bible lecture on 'God is love.'" Modern churchgoers are not surprised or taken aback today by the notion of the interactive service, occasions when audience participation is encouraged— often to help make a point in a way that is memorable. But in the staid dissenting tradition of 1870s England, this was a new thing under the sun. Moody created a stir among the eight hundred souls who heard him that afternoon at the Corn Exchange. More important, they left talking about a theological concept too often given short shrift in sermons of the time: God is love. Here was an American friend who was winsome and earnest in telling that good news.[20]

Meanwhile, in answer to a request to use local chapels in which to hold evening meetings, Moody and Sankey received the news that two Wesleyan, a Baptist, and a Congregational church were placed at their disposal.[21] This was encouraging, but while the meetings subsequently held in these venues were well attended, there appeared to be little outward result in the way of people coming forward to make a commitment to Christ. Chapel attendance was an expected thing at this time. People would come if a meeting was scheduled, and there seemed little to say except they came out of a sense of convention: it was what was done.[22]

But underneath the surface of this outward conformity, God was at work—touching the hearts of men, women, and children. Moody, Sankey, and Bennett did not as yet know this, but signs of something special unfolding would not be long in coming.[23]

All the while, Moody and his coworkers continued earnestly in prayer. One English colleague, the Reverend F. B. Meyer, remembered it all—as the following excerpts from a letter he wrote many years later attest. It affords a near view of events as they unfolded and lends an immediacy that makes the first days of this remarkable preaching tour come alive.

I have known Mr. Moody ever since a memorable Monday morning in 1873. I can see him now, standing up to lead the first noon prayer-meeting in a small, ill-lit room in Coney Street, York, little realizing that it was the seed-germ of a mighty harvest, and that a movement was beginning that would culminate in a few months in Free Assembly Hall, Edinburgh, and ultimately in the Agricultural Hall and the Royal Opera House, London. It was the birth-time of new conceptions of ministry, new methods of work, new inspirations and hopes.[24]

What an inspiration when this great and noble soul first broke into my life! I was a young pastor then, in the old city of York, and bound rather rigidly by the chains of conventionalism. Such had been my training, and such might have been my career. But here was a revelation of a new ideal. The first characteristic of Mr. Moody's that struck me was that he was so absolutely unconventional and natural. That a piece of work had generally been done after a certain method would probably be the reason why he would set about it in some fresh and unexpected way. That the new method startled people was the greater reason for continuing with it, if only it drew them to the Gospel. But there was never the slightest approach to irreverence, fanaticism, or extravagance; everything was in perfect accord with a rare common sense, a directness of method, a simplicity and transparency of aim, which were as attractive as they were fruitful.[25]

The first ten days of his meetings were only moderately successful, and he gladly accepted my invitation to come to the chapel where I ministered, and there we had a fortnight of most blessed and memorable meetings. The little vestry there—how vividly I remember it!—was the scene of our long and earnest prayers as we knelt around the leather-covered table in the middle of the room. Two Presbyterian students, brothers, from Dr. McKay's church in Hull, often used to pray with us, and I remember that Mr. Moody, at the great Free Trade Hall, Manchester, referred to that little room as the fountain from which the river of blessing for the whole country had sprung.[26]

Many recollections of those days come back as I write: How in the midst of tea at home Mr. Moody suddenly felt that he should preach his afterward famous sermon on Heaven, and started off on a three miles' walk to fetch his notes; how Mr. Sankey went over to see Mr. Rees, of Sunderland, the sailor-preacher, of whom I had spoken to them, and proved his singing powers in the little back parlor of W. D. Longstaff, to the entire satisfaction of both minister and elder; how we had our all-day meeting, the first of its kind in England; and how the fire of God burnt hot in all our hearts. Ah, blessed days! that will live as long as memory endures.[27]

The first public report of the meetings in York appeared in the form of a letter from George Bennett printed in the July 10 issue of a periodical called *The Christian*. Bennett wrote:

On Sunday morning, June 22d, Mr. Moody preached in Salem Congregational Chapel to Christian workers; in the afternoon, in the Corn Exchange, to about a thousand persons, and in the evening in Wesley Chapel . . . Every evening during the following week Bible lectures were delivered in various chapels . . . Formality and apathy are to a great extent dissipated, and Christians have been led to pray and work for the conversion of sinners.[28]

During the past week the Lord has greatly blessed us in the ingathering of souls. On Sabbath day, June 29th, Mr.

Moody preached in two other chapels, and also twice in the Corn Exchange, to audiences numbering about a thousand each. Every week evening service is preceded by a service of song, conducted by Mr. Moody's co-laborer, Mr. Sankey, whose hymns, tunes, and voice . . . have drawn and impressed many. Mr. Moody preaches the Gospel and Mr. Sankey sings it. Prayer-meetings have been held every noon at the rooms of the Young Men's Christian Association, and many there have offered themselves and others for the prayers of God's people.[29]

Though this is the summer season, and we were under a disadvantage in consequence (through the miscarriage of letters to and from Mr. Moody) of not having notice, and, therefore, were unprepared for his visit, when Mr. Moody dropped down on us on the Saturday morning, arrangements were made and bills printed all in a few hours, and from the first the Lord has greatly blessed our brothers' labors in the strengthening and stimulating of Christians and in the bringing of many out of darkness into light; their visit will long be remembered in this city. The congregations have from the first been increasingly large; all denominations have opened their chapels and given us their presence and help. Many of the clergy have also heartily bidden them "God-speed."[30]

P.S.—Sunday evening, 11pm. Just before posting this, let me add that this afternoon a large chapel was filled to hear Moody; a deep impression was made. I have just come from the evening service, where every aisle and standing place, the vestries and lobbies, even the pulpit stairs, were crowded nearly half an hour before the evening service commenced. The Holy Spirit worked mightily, sinners in all positions in life sought the Lord earnestly, and Christian brothers and sisters of the Church of England, Friends, and of every denomination, were constrained without invitation to speak and pray with them. I don't know how many, but over fifty gave their hearts to Christ.[31]

Writing again from York on July 14, Bennett reported that the American evangelists were still there and that every meeting during the week just passed had been attended with great blessing. "One distinguishing feature of our brother's meetings," he said,

is the Bible lectures which he gives on such subjects as "The Blood of Christ," "Walking with God," etc. The passages of Scripture are previously selected and read out by friends in various parts of the audience. The chapel was crowded long before the service last evening, and many sought and found the Saviour . . . Pray that these meetings may become an institution in this city and be greatly used of God in the binding together of Christians of every name, in the deepening of their spiritual life.[32]

Each public service was followed by an inquiry meeting, which at first was considered a novelty, but gradually became a great power in the work. Mr. Moody's manner of expounding the Scripture at once attracted attention. The Bible readings, which he had given in Brooklyn and other cities, were continued with great effect. Believers were aroused to a new interest in the Sacred Word. Bibles were seen at every meeting and new methods of Bible study were suggested.[33]

The first all-day meeting Moody held in England was arranged with F. B. Meyer as they walked up and down Coney Street, York. It began at 11:00 a.m. and lasted six hours, and an evening service followed. From its novelty it attracted great attention, and it commended itself heartily to all who attended the services. First, there was an hour for confession and prayer; second, an hour for praise; third, a promise meeting, which consisted of testimonies on the part of believers to the fulfilment of promises in their own experiences; fourth, a witness meeting, which was a series of public confessions of Christ by young converts; fifth, a Bible lecture by Mr. Moody; and, finally, a communion service conducted by Mr. Moody and four ministers.[34]

After five weeks of meetings in York, several hundred people had been converted. Many others testified to a deepening of their spiritual life that left them forever changed. Moody and Sankey were now at the eve of departing for a series of meetings scheduled for Sunderland.[35] The whole of Great Britain, it seemed, now lay open to the work they had come to do.

9

THE GREAT GATHERING

Both these brethren are genuine to the backbone.
They are as disinterested as they are zealous, and their
zeal is extraordinary. Mr. Moody is the "Mercurius"of
the pair. Mr. Sankey is not the "Jupiter," but the
"Orpheus." The former is not eloquent, but very
fluent; not poetical or rhetorical, but he never talks
twaddle and seldom utters a sentence that is not well
worth hearing.[1]

—Arthur Rees

I n ways that no one could have foreseen, the preaching tour
that commenced at York grew in time to become a two-
year crusade that fostered a nationwide spiritual renewal
in Great Britain. No one had ever seen anything quite like it.
Many marveled that a rough-hewn American was at the heart
of it—not least D. L. Moody himself. Space does not allow for
an exhaustive account of all that unfolded, but some important
highlights and milestones can be touched on.

For a start, this first great British preaching tour was not without opposition or controversy—at least for a time after Moody and Sankey left York. After a five-week campaign in Sunderland, and additional preaching tours before ever-increasing crowds throughout Yorkshire and Northumberland in the cities like Newcastle-on-Tyne and Carlisle, Moody and Sankey moved on to Scotland at the behest of a committee of Christians based in Edinburgh.[2]

It was at this time that controversy reared its head in a manner no one could have foreseen. The facts were as follows. For reasons unknown, a Scottish lawyer in Chicago had conceived a deep antipathy toward Moody. He now sent a scurrilous letter to a prominent clergyman in Scotland leveling scattershot charges relating to Moody's business dealings and religious character. The charges, unsupported and baseless, were that Moody had sold information regarding the interest of one of his employers to a business rival; and, further, that he was insincere in his attitude toward some religious doctrines many Scots held in deep reverence. Whatever the specifics of these charges were, the intent in leveling them was clear: to destroy Moody personally as well as his preaching ministry in the United Kingdom.[3]

The scurrilous letter was widely distributed in manuscript copies in places where it would do the greatest possible harm and where it would be most difficult to counteract its influence. At last a copy fell into the hands of the Edinburgh Committee that had invited Moody to come. Steps were now taken to ascertain the truth or falsity of the statements made.[4]

Moody, as his son Will later wrote,

was deeply exercised over the letter for the sake of the work in Scotland, although perfectly conscious of his rectitude. He trusted his reputation implicitly to his Heavenly Father and demanded that the committee who had invited him to Edinburgh give the matter a thorough investigation. The Rev. John Kelman, of Free St. John's, Leith, the secretary of the Edinburgh Committee, and the man who had gone to Newcastle to see Mr. Moody's work, and who was in a large measure responsible for his visit to Scotland, sent a copy of the letter to Mr. Farwell in Chicago, saying: "The friends of religion who have been associated in Christian work with Mr. Moody in this country are anxious that there should be a thorough investigation of the truth or falsity of these charges. I have been requested to apply to you in the hope that you would be kind enough to furnish me at your earliest convenience with whatever information you can obtain as to the facts in the case."[5]

Farwell sprang into action and lost no time in drafting a letter that fully laid everyone's concerns to rest. He then did more, for when his letter was forwarded to Kelman in Scotland it had been signed by thirty-five clergymen, educators, editors, and secretaries who had known Moody and his work in Chicago. Addressed to the Edinburgh Committee as a whole, it fully refuted the charges leveled against Moody and read in part:

We, the undersigned pastors of the city of Chicago, learning that the Christian character of D. L. Moody has been attacked,

for the purpose of destroying his influence as an evangelist in Scotland, hereby certify that his labors in the Young Men's Christian Association, and as an evangelist in this city and elsewhere, according to the best information we can get, have been evangelical and Christian in the highest sense of those terms; and we do not hesitate to commend him as an earnest Christian worker, worthy of the confidence of our Scotch and English brethren, with whom he is now laboring, believing that the Master will be honored by them in receiving him among them as a co-laborer in the vineyard of the Lord.[6]

Will Moody later wrote that it was "two or three months before this slander was run down and killed." Yet in the end, when Moody had been more than cleared of all charges, the result was that he now had a character above reproach in Scotland and beyond. Given this, Moody, Sankey, and their wives might well have concluded that what the Scottish lawyer in Chicago had meant for evil, God had meant for good.[7]

~

These were the unlikely circumstances that gave rise to what was later called "the awakening in Edinburgh." As Will Moody reported, along with the Edinburgh meetings, services were also held in Leith. The meetings in Leith proved crucial, for due to the large shipping interests of the city, the meetings attracted people from almost every part of the world. Many seafaring men attended the services, and in consequence, the message of the meetings Moody and Sankey held not only extended

throughout the great population of Scotland but was carried in ships around the world.[8] Thousands may have heard the gospel in Edinburgh and Leith, and for this all concerned were deeply thankful. But the ripple effect was international in scope. Something extraordinary was beginning to take shape.

≈

Moody and Sankey moved on to Glasgow after the Edinburgh mission closed. In fact, preparations for this eventual move had begun as soon as the Edinburgh work had started. In the middle of December 1873, a meeting was held in Glasgow to arrange for the visit of the Americans, which was attended by more than a hundred ministers and laymen of all the evangelical churches.[9]

At the first of a series of union prayer meetings in St. George's Established Church on January 5, Moody spoke briefly, returning to Edinburgh for the evening meeting. After beginning their work in Glasgow, he returned to Edinburgh two or three times to assist in special meetings. Berwick-on-Tweed, Melrose, and Dundee were also visited, and meetings lasting a few days each were conducted there after the Edinburgh mission closed.[10]

The Glasgow meetings had been going on uninterrupted for more than a month when Moody and Sankey arrived there on February 7. They began their work the following morning. At nine o'clock a stirring meeting of Sabbath-school teachers was held in the city hall, attended by about three thousand. The evening evangelistic service was held at six thirty, but more than an hour before that time the city hall was crowded, and

the great multitude outside were drafted off to the three nearest churches, which were soon filled.[11]

The next day a prayer meeting began in the morning in the United Presbyterian Church. Dr. Horatius Bonar described the meetings that were held during this time:

> There have been not a few awakened of late, and the interest is deepening. The ministers of all denominations take part most cordially. Men are coming from great distances to ask the way of life, awakened to this concern by no directly human means, but evidently by the Holy Spirit, who is breathing over the land. It is such a time as we have never had in Scotland before. The same old Gospel as of aforetime is preached to all men: Christ who was made sin for us, Christ the substitute, Christ's blood, Christ's righteousness, Christ crucified; the power of God and the wisdom of God unto salvation; but now the Gospel is preached with the Holy Ghost sent down from Heaven.[12]

"From Glasgow as a centre," Will Moody wrote,

> occasional meetings were arranged in adjoining towns, and Helensburg, Greenock, and Paisley were visited, while the ministers of Glasgow and other cities took the regular meetings during the absence of Mr. Moody. On Thursday, April 16th, a convention of ministers, office-bearers, and other Christians from all parts of Scotland and the North of England was held in the Crystal Palace Botanical Gardens.

Five thousand people were present, the larger proportion being men. Professor Charteris, of Edinburgh, read a paper showing how the revival movement could be advanced and directed into the ordinary church channels. Professor Fairburn, of the Free College, spoke upon the great doctrines which had been emphasized during the meetings. Dr. Cairns, of Berwick, Mr. Van Meter, of Rome, and others took part. One of the most impressive gatherings during this mission was a meeting held in the Kibble Crystal Palace especially for warehouse girls, of whom there are probably more than twelve thousand in the city. Tickets were issued, and while five thousand were seated in the building and several hundred standing, outside was a crowd of more than a thousand girls.[13]

On the following evening the meeting was for young men, when nearly six thousand were brought together. A service was held for children also, and another for young women. The final meeting was held in the Botanical Gardens on the following Sunday. Mr. Sankey found his way into the building and began the service with six or seven thousand, who were crushed together there, but so great was the crowd outside, estimated at twenty or thirty thousand people, that Mr. Moody himself could not get inside.[14]

Standing on the coachman's box of the carriage in which he was driven, he asked the members of the choir to sing. They found a place for themselves on the roof of a low shed near the building, and after they had sung Mr. Moody preached for an hour on "Immediate Salvation." So distinct was his voice that the great crowd could hear him without difficulty. The evening was beautiful, the air calm, the sun near its setting; the deep green foliage of the trees that enclosed the grounds framed the scene. Writing of this, a witness said: "We thought of the days of Whitefield, of such a scene as that mentioned in his life, when, in 1753 at Glasgow, twenty thousand souls hung on his lips as he bade them farewell. Here there were thirty thousand eager hearers, for by this time the thousands within the Crystal Palace had come out, though their numbers quietly melting into the main body did not make a very perceptible addition to the crowd; and many onlookers who knew something of such gatherings were inclined to estimate the number much higher."[15]

After the sermon Moody asked all those who wished to attend the inquiry meeting to enter the palace. Those who could remain were requested to gather in the neighboring church, Kelvinside, for prayer. Within minutes the Crystal Palace was filled, and when Moody asked those who wished to place their faith in Christ to stand, two thousand people rose to their feet.[16]

≈

It was inevitable after such a long and successful stay in Scotland, with meetings such as the ones just described, that Moody, Sankey, and an ever-increasing company of British co-laborers would turn their thoughts toward the great metropolitan centers of England.

The campaign to reach people for Christ in these cities

began in earnest early in 1875. In January of that year, Moody and Sankey held a meeting in Birmingham's Bingley Hall that met with great success. It left a deep impression on one Anglican clergyman, who wrote: "Such a chance of guiding souls comes only once in a lifetime."[17]

A series of meetings in Liverpool that commenced in February were the scene of a serious threat against Moody's life. Prior to the start of these meetings at a massive auditorium specially constructed of timber for Moody and Sankey's arrival, Moody was seized with an unshakable premonition of danger. Acting on this, extra security measures were taken and great caution was exercised throughout the duration of the campaign. Moody's concerns were proved right when, following one meeting, the police told him they had just apprehended a madman convinced that Confederate ghosts were goading him to murder Moody—the Yankee preacher.[18]

As winter passed into spring, people throughout England were coming to faith in the thousands. This was due in no small measure to "the tremendous wave of prayer" that persisted throughout Moody and Sankey's tour. Moody was always insistent that prayer was crucial to the success of any great endeavor for God.[19]

No less crucial to the success with which Moody was heard was the way he proclaimed it. People left the halls where he spoke feeling as though he had come alongside them at their point of need. As Dr. R. W. Dale of Carr's Lane Congregational Church in Birmingham phrased it, Moody had a gift for speaking with "perfect naturalness. He talks in a perfectly unconstrained and straightforward way, just as he would talk to half a dozen old friends at this fireside."[20]

Building on this thought, Moody's distinguished biographer John Pollock has observed: "In an age of ponderous sermons when [Charles] Spurgeon, most popular of all preachers, mouthed rolling periods, piled metaphor upon metaphor, Moody merely chatted, 'to thirteen thousand as thirteen' on what the Bible showed him. He made it alive in the context of every day."[21]

Moody's reputation for moral probity also bolstered the cause of the gospel and engendered great respect—even from those not especially religious. For those inclined to label him as a P. T. Barnum of the pulpit—and such charges of hucksterism and profiteering were leveled at Moody (some even charged that Barnum was bankrolling the British campaign)—his conduct and the accountability mechanisms he insisted on were a potent corrective. In an age like our own, when scandals routinely seem to destroy ministers and ministries, the nature of how Moody's ministry conducted itself shines the brighter.

This could be seen most vividly in the controversy surrounding the sales of *Sacred Songs and Solos*, a collection of the songs (many written by Sankey and a gifted colleague, Philip Bliss) featured during the revival meetings. As requests for the publication of these hymns mounted, Moody took it upon himself to arrange for their publication in book form with the firm of Morgan and Scott.[22]

The book, to which new songs were periodically added, became a runaway bestseller and generated huge sums of money. It was at this time that the allegations of hucksterism surfaced. Moody and Sankey were said to be enriching themselves, bankrolling funds as quickly as they came in.[23]

Moody took steps to stop that rumor dead in its tracks. During a large public meeting of ministers and other leaders, he stated explicitly that all royalties from the hymnbook, then in the hands of his publishers, together with funds that might afterward accrue, would be placed in the hands of a committee of well-known businessmen.[24]

The matter came to a close in the following way. At the close of the London campaign, shortly before Moody and Sankey were scheduled to return to America, the royalty statement of Morgan and Scott showed that about £7,000 ($35,000 in 1875 dollars) had come in—an amount equal to $280,000 in today's currency.[25] Moody subsequently sent word to the committee he had asked to oversee the dispersal of these funds that the money was at their disposal, to be used as they might see fit.[26]

They decided to devote the entire sum to help rebuild the church Moody had established in Chicago, destroyed during the Great Chicago Fire. There was a need, since plans to rebuild the church had been thwarted during the financial panic of 1873–74. Only one story of the church had been completed, capped with a temporary roof. When the London committee learned this was the case, they forwarded the money to Chicago to facilitate the rebuilding. Will Moody said that this decision resulted in the completion of "the splendid edifice at Chicago Avenue and La Salle Street, which has been a centre of spiritual activity for more than twenty-five years." It was completed and dedicated free of debt.[27]

The story of the hymnbooks had a sequel after Moody and Sankey returned to America. In August 1875 it became necessary to arrange for the publication of a new collection of hymns, composed largely of those that had been used throughout the United Kingdom. After some discussion, the title *Gospel Hymns and Sacred Songs* was adopted. It became wildly popular, and large numbers were sold during great meetings held in Philadelphia, New York, Chicago, and Boston.[28]

All the while, new hymns were constantly being written. And so it was natural that subsequent compilations appeared. *Gospel Hymns, No. 1* was followed by Nos. 2, 3, 4, 5, and 6. The royalties from these books were at first paid to a committee of prominent businessmen of Philadelphia, Chicago, and New York, of which William E. Dodge, of New York, was chairman. Dodge and his colleagues then distributed the funds that had accrued to benefit religious, philanthropic, and educational initiatives in many parts of the United States.[29]

When Moody later founded the Northfield and Mount Hermon schools, funds from the sales of hymnbooks covered the cost of building East Hall, a dormitory at the young ladies' seminary— and also Stone Hall, a recitation hall at the same institution. Additional funds were used to construct Recitation Hall at Mount Hermon. As late as 1900, royalties were being paid directly to the trustees of the schools of Northfield and Mount Hermon.[30]

William Dodge's recollection of how this hymnbook philanthropic initiative commenced is worth noting:

On [Mr. Moody's] return to America, he invited me to visit Northfield to confer with him on [a] subject which he felt to be of great importance. I met there Mr. Sankey and Mr. Bliss, and found a most delightful and unusual spirit of Christian self-sacrifice on their part. They were willing to contribute their own hymns and tunes and the copyrights which they held, and joined with Mr. Moody in giving up all possible claim to any benefits which might arise from their publication. Mr. Moody urged me to act as trustee, to arrange with the publishers for a royalty, and to receive any money which might come from this source and distribute it at my discretion for religious and benevolent purposes. I declined to act alone, but promised Mr. Moody that if two other gentlemen were selected I would gladly serve with them, and suggested the names of George H. Stuart, of Philadelphia, and John V. Farwell, of Chicago; a board of trustees was thus formed.[31]

Dodge, Stuart, and Farwell oversaw the disbursal of funds through September 1885 to various religious and educational institutions. The amount thus distributed amounted to a considerable fortune: $357,388.64 (or nearly three million dollars in today's currency).[32] Following this, they decided that it would be "wise and right that [since] the schools at Northfield had become so firmly established, and were doing such great good, the entire royalties of these books should be turned over to the trustees of these schools, and this was accordingly done under careful legal advice."[33]

One final word should be given here before returning to an

overview of the London campaign—Moody and Sankey's final campaign in Britain. During all the years that funds from the sales of the hymnbooks were secured and distributed, neither Moody nor Sankey had any fixed income. Sankey, in particular, "had given up copyrights that would have brought him in a large sum yearly and opportunities to hold musical institutes and conventions which would have added largely to his income."[34]

When, years later, the time came for Will Moody to close the trust that had been created to distribute funds from the sale of hymnbooks, he sought legal counsel as to the best course to pursue. "After getting full legal advice," he wrote,

> I submitted the opinions to a lawyer of very high national reputation—the leader of the bar in New York in all matters of consultation. He was greatly interested in the form of the trust, though he had but little sympathy with the religious work. He gave a large amount of time and thought to the matter, and after giving his opinion I asked him to be kind enough to send me a memorandum, so that I could personally send him a check, which I supposed would necessarily be a large one. He told me that under no possible circumstance would he accept a cent; that the unselfishness and splendid quality of men who could make such a sacrifice was a revelation of human nature that made him feel better disposed toward mankind.[35]

The capstone of Moody and Sankey's mission to Britain was the four months of the London mission of 1875. Its impact can be seen most starkly through the following statistics: In Camberwell Hall, 60 meetings were attended by 480,000 people; in Victoria Hall, 45 meetings were attended by 400,000; in the Royal Haymarket Opera House, 60 meetings were attended by 330,000; in Bow Road Hall, 60 meetings were attended by 600,000; and in Agricultural Hall, 60 meetings were attended by 720,000. In all, some 285 meetings were attended by 2,530,000 people. The expenses of the mission came to just over £28,396, nearly all of which was covered by donation before the close of the meetings.[36]

Ireland, Scotland, and England—all had been deeply stirred by spiritual renewal. Moody and Sankey, so dismayed by what they had encountered upon their arrival in Britain in 1873, had been much blessed of God. Nothing like the tour they had undertaken had been seen since the days of the Wesleys and Whitefield, and perhaps not even then.

In the years to come, Moody would crisscross North America countless times and return to Britain—preaching to people in the tens of millions throughout the remainder of his life—but nothing was quite like this first great preaching tour—when D. L. Moody truly became, by grace and in ways no one could have foreseen, God's herald in the gilded age. With him every step of the way was Ira Sankey—Moody preached the gospel and Sankey sang it into life. They were a team like no other.

10

THE SEMINARY AT NORTHFIELD

Those of us who knew Mr. Moody well remember how he loved beautiful things. The song of the brook was music to his soul; the coming of the leaves and flowers of spring was a parable; and his own dear Northfield was beloved by him to the end. He was perfectly happy when driving about through the beauties of the surrounding country.[1]

When Mr. Moody returned to Northfield after his evangelistic tour of Great Britain, he went home to Northfield to rest. With his eyes sharpened by travel, and with his usual alert observance of the needs of those about him, he conceived a plan of making possible education for girls who were born to the unstimulating routine of farm life. The [origin] of Northfield Seminary lay in this conception. . . . The school now numbers about four hundred pupils, its graduates being admitted to Wellesley, Smith and other high-grade institutions.[2]

—J. Wilbur Chapman

The Northfield and Mount Hermon schools were two cherished facets of D. L. Moody's educational dream to aid the underprivileged. The Northfield Seminary, the first of these two institutions to be established, has a remarkable story connected with it—one forever associated with Moody's beloved younger brother, Samuel. Recounted by Moody's eldest son, Will, it unfolded as follows.[3]

One day, sometime prior to 1876, Moody was returning to Northfield from travels elsewhere. Driving with his brother Samuel over one of the mountain roads near the village, they passed an isolated cottage, far from town or any neighbor. Sitting in the doorway were a mother and two daughters braiding straw hats.

Moody decided to stop for a few moments to visit, perhaps to rest and water his team of horses. As he and Samuel talked with the two daughters, they learned that their father was bedridden with paralysis and could do nothing to support his family. The burden of providing for the family had fallen to the two girls. They were able to make ends meet but had no time left to pursue their schooling—something they ardently wished to do, since their ailing father was well educated and had stirred a deep desire within them to learn.

Both Moodys were greatly moved by this story. Because they had been reared in Northfield themselves amid poverty, and without a father, they knew only too well that for every family like this with daughters who wished to learn, there were many others similarly circumstanced. It moved them to see these young women consigned to lonely lives of toil with no hope of something better.

Samuel felt particularly burdened. In subsequent discussions with his elder brother, he spoke often of the idea of doing something to change things for the girls they had met, and others like them.

Samuel Moody's role in the founding of the Northfield Seminary, though brief and of a behind-the-scenes nature, is noteworthy. Indeed, it is worth taking a few moments to speak of the special relationship the two brothers shared.

D. L. Moody was particularly close to this brother, the youngest in his family. Samuel was not strong physically, and so his activities upon reaching adulthood were somewhat circumscribed. He read law for a time and gave every indication of making a good attorney.

The personalities of the two brothers were also much the same. Like his elder brother, Samuel was fond of young people and was instrumental in starting a debating society in Northfield. At the same time, he constantly regretted the limited opportunities the local schools afforded his twin sister to develop her mind and often expressed a wish that something more substantial might be made available.

Samuel's health, never robust, eventually gave way—resulting in his untimely death in 1876. But before his passing, he had bequeathed one lasting legacy through his brother D. L. to generations of young women. And Moody resolved to do as his younger brother had suggested. He would found a school "to put such educational advantages within reach of girls living among the New England hills as would fit them for a broader sphere in life than they could otherwise hope for."[4]

Another channel that influenced the founding of the Northfield Seminary came through Moody's friendship with Henry F. Durant of Boston. They had known each other since the 1860s, and during a preaching campaign that Moody held in Boston in 1878, he stayed in Durant's home. Just three years before, Durant had realized a long-cherished dream when Wellesley College (initially called Wellesley Female Seminary) opened its doors to receive its first students in September 1875. During Moody's stay with him in Boston, Durant's conversation centered on the plans he was pursuing for his new school. Moody was deeply impressed by all that he saw and heard. The two men visited the college several times together, and Moody later became one of Wellesley's trustees.

Uniquely, Durant believed it was central to the educational mission for young women that, in additional to pursuing advanced studies, they also be required to assist in the maintenance of their school through the performance of domestic chores within the dormitories in which they lived. This would, he thought, help foster character development, teaching the young women who entered Wellesley of the need to give something back in return for the educational privileges they had received. There was a practical side to this to be sure, but it was the principle of a grateful return for privileges received that lay at the heart of Durant's thinking in this regard.

This was entirely in keeping with Wellesley's commitment to keeping Christ and the Scriptures at the center of Wellesley's educational mission. Christ had shown by His example how important it was to serve others. Seen in this light, Durant was encouraging the students at Wellesley to take part in "service projects"—now so often a staple of the educational experience in American colleges and universities.

Moody took note of all this and heartily concurred. When he began to pursue the establishment of Northfield Seminary in earnest, he had determined that he would in many respects follow Durant's lead.

Things got going in 1878, though not in a way that Moody could have foreseen.

In the autumn of that year, Moody was at his home in Northfield, discussing the ideas of a school for girls with H. N. F. Marshall, of Boston. As they talked, Moody saw that the owner of sixteen acres of adjoining land to his own was passing by. Thinking it providential, Moody approached his neighbor and asked him if he would sell his land. The neighbor said he was willing and named a price, whereupon Moody and Marshall invited the man into Moody's home, "made out the papers, and before the owner had recovered from his surprise, the land had passed out of his hands."[5]

As Will Moody recalled, the land that would soon become the initial physical footprint of campus of the Northfield Seminary was acquired in quick succession. "Three or four adjoining lots were bought out in the course of a year, all without their respective owners realizing that their barren farm-lands had any special value. These purchases increased the estate to one hundred acres, the greater part being bare, sandy hillocks, useless even for pasturage, but suitably located, and commanding a pleasing view of the Connecticut Valley."[6]

It had all been a characteristic turn of events, not unlike Moody's initial desire to assist the two young women he had met in the isolated cottage. Now, in the fall of 1878, he saw an opportunity when his neighbor walked by. He seized it, setting in motion a series of events that made the Northfield Seminary a reality. And here, words he so often said bear repeating: "I am a man of impulse. The best things I have ever done have been decided on the impulse."[7]

≈

In the spring of 1879, construction of a recitation hall intended for one hundred students commenced. Will Moody fondly remembered how it all began:

> With characteristic promptness and energy, [Father] could not wait for a dormitory to be built, but altered his own house to accommodate the students. Instead of the eight pupils as expected, twenty-five appeared. With these, the Northfield Seminary for Young Women was formally opened on November 3, 1879, classes being held in the dining-room of [our] home until the recitation hall was completed the following December.[8]

The setting was a world away from the abandoned saloon where Moody had begun to teach the children of Little Hell—a world away from the squalor and violence of the inner city— but the principle was much the same: young people in need being given opportunities they would never have otherwise. Moody and his wife, Emma, were breaking new ground for the kingdom's sake, in ways that were decidedly outside the conventional box. It is often said that charity begins at home. So it did in those first days of the Northfield Seminary.

Among the first students who met together in the dining room were the two girls Moody had seen braiding straw hats outside their mountain home. They excelled as students and were models of all that the Northfield Seminary sought to be and perpetuate.

Ground was broken for the first dormitory, East Hall, in April 1880. It was completed in August of the following year and used during the first ten days of September to accommodate those who attended what would in time become a cherished feature of life in Northfield: the first Christian Workers' Conference. On the last day of this conference, at the close of one of the morning meetings, Moody invited those present into the chapel of East Hall for the purpose of dedicating the building. After the singing of hymns, Moody addressed those who had gathered:

> You know that the Lord laid it upon my heart some time ago
> to organize a school for young women in the humbler walks
> of life, who never would get a Christian education but for a
> school like this. I talked about this plan of mine to friends,
> until a number of them gave money to start the school. Some
> thought I ought to make it for boys and girls, but I thought
> that if I wished to send my daughter away to school I should

prefer to send her to an institution for girls only. I have hoped
that money might be given for a boys' school, and now a gentleman who has been here for the last ten days has become
interested in my plans, and has given twenty-five thousand
dollars toward a school for boys.

And now as we dedicate this building to God, I want to
read you the motto of this school.

Then, turning to Isaiah 27:3, he read: "I the Lord do keep
it; I will water it every moment: lest any hurt it, I will keep it
night and day."[9]

Even as Henry Durant had sought to place Christ and the
Scriptures at the center of student life at Wellesley, Moody now
sought to do the same at the Northfield Seminary. He did so in a
way entirely in keeping with the son of a mason. A copy of the
Scriptures was placed in the cornerstone of each of the school
buildings as they were built. This was, Will Moody wrote,
"symbolic of the place that God's Word holds in the life of the
schools. It [was] indeed, foundation, cornerstone, and capstone
of [Father's] whole system. He recognized that all studies have
their value; but believed their importance is increased if pursued in right relation to central truths."[10]

～

During the first twenty years of its existence—that is, until D. L.
Moody's death in December 1899—the Northfield Seminary
featured a curriculum that was progressive in many ways.
Students could pursue one of three courses of study. The college

preparatory course enabled the student to enter any of the leading colleges on certificate. The general course offered the same advantages in Latin, but afforded more freedom in the choice of electives. The English course, by omitting the study of languages, provided an opportunity for more extended work in sciences, history, and literature. In all three courses of study, students were "stimulated to independent thought and investigation."[11]

Extracurricular life at Northfield Seminary in those early years took full advantage of the natural beauty of the village and its surroundings. The quaint cadences of Victorian prose captured this institutional emphasis: "It is not the idea of the Seminary to pay exclusive attention to the training of the mind and soul, but rather to develop a symmetrical womanhood. At least half an hour of outdoor exercise must be taken daily by all."[12]

Nearby Wanamaker Lake became a center of outdoor activity. Skaters would gather there in the winter months, while afternoons from June through September were spent boating. "Long walks and climbs" were also favorite pastimes undertaken in and around Northfield. When the weather was inclement, students exercised indoors in a handsome new gymnasium, where basketball and tennis were favorite sports.[13]

In the first years of the Northfield Seminary, the Young Women's Christian Association (YWCA) actively supervised "the various departments of Christian activity." An outgrowth of D. L. Moody's long association with the YMCA, the involvement of the YWCA in life at Northfield was undertaken with a view toward fostering faith and the pursuit of opportunities for service that ought to flow out from it. Will Moody recalled that the work of the YWCA at the school "kept students in sympathy with the larger movements to make the world better."[14]

In June 1899 the Northfield Seminary celebrated its twentieth anniversary. By this time, its enrollment had risen to nearly four hundred students, with a staff of teachers and matrons numbering thirty-nine. The campus had also grown considerably, now consisting of "five hundred acres of land, nine dormitories, a gymnasium, library, recitation hall, auditorium, and farm buildings."[15]

It was all a sight that gladdened D. L. Moody's heart. His faith had been the source of all that was good in his life. Now a vibrant school existed that could commend that faith to young women and give them the education he never had.

THE BOYS OF MOUNT HERMON

When I was pastor of his church, I brought [Mr. Moody] several such [boys]. He fixed his piercing eye upon them and said, "You want an education? What do you want it for? To do good, did you say? Are you in earnest? Well, get ready and start for Northfield tomorrow; I will pay your expenses." And then his great brown eyes, lit up with an almost maternal tenderness, would follow them to the door as if he were dreaming of their future.[1]

—Charles F. Goss

N o sooner," Will Moody wrote,

was the [Northfield] Seminary under way than a corresponding school for boys suggested itself. [The] Mount Hermon School for Young Men was therefore started on similar principles. The first purchase of property was made in November 1879, when a farm of one hundred and seventy-five acres was secured by [my father]. When, a little later, Mr. Hiram Camp, of New Haven, Connecticut, agreed to contribute $25,000, some adjoining land was bought, and the school started with an estate of about two hundred and seventy-five acres and two farmhouses. At Mr. Camp's suggestion the name Mount Hermon was adopted, *"for there the Lord commanded the blessing, even life for evermore."* (Psalm 133:3).[2]

Two years after the first land was purchased for the Mount Hermon School, on May 4, 1881, the first group of boys arrived to begin their studies. They were age eight, while the oldest boys were twelve. Moody's initial thought was that needy boys of this age could be given "home life and help, of which they knew little." However, a flood of applications from "young men whose early education had for various reasons been meager" prompted a change in admission age policy three years after Mount Hermon opened its doors. The rationale was that "younger boys had more opportunities to secure schooling elsewhere than the older class of applicants." Also, a wide range in age created unnecessary challenges by way of maintaining discipline. Therefore, the age limit for admission was raised, and it was decided to accept no applicants under the age of sixteen.[3]

From the start, Moody wanted Mount Hermon to be a different kind of school. As his son Will remembered,

[Father] had not mere charity in view; hence his schools [did] not offer their privileges gratuitously. But he knew that raw material of the most promising kind is often to be found among people of little or no [means], who cannot afford the usual expense of academy life, and in order to open the doors to such, the annual fee of the Northfield schools was fixed at $100 a year, or about half the cost of board and tuition. [Father] proposed to give tuition and training free to such as would provide their own living expenses.[4]

One of the most unique ways that Mount Hermon bore the stamp of Moody's character could be seen in the policy of manual labor that was adopted there. As instituted, it required that "every student, big or little, senior or preparatorian, must do a certain amount of manual labor every day, the work being adapted to his physical ability, but entirely regardless of any social standing." Again, this anticipates the emphasis on "service projects" that have become commonplace today; but so far as Moody was concerned, there was something more behind the practice of requiring students to perform manual labor: he wished to keep any notions of "aristocracy" from taking root among the students. The importance of establishing a sense of common purpose and fellowship within an environment of shared responsibilities mattered deeply to him. It was a vital part of a boy's education, one—as Will Moody recalled— "[Father] and the teachers . . . regarded as valuable as that of the classroom."[5]

The daily program boys followed in those early years of

the Mount Hermon School was "tolled out by bells." Glancing through it, one can see that their days were full from early morning to the turning out of the lights at night. At 6:00 a.m., the rising bell sounded. Fifteen minutes later, a student officer toured the rooms to make sure no one had forgotten (or refused) to get up. Twenty minutes, from 6:30 to 6:50 were set aside for "private devotions"—by which was meant a time for personal prayer and the reading of Scripture. Breakfast followed at 7:00, and the time from 7:40 to 11:50 was reserved for "study and recitation."[6]

Chapel exercises commenced at 11:55, usually lasting about half an hour. Dinner was served at 12:30 p.m., followed by a period of "work-time" that lasted from 1:20 to 3:20. After this, one hour was set aside for "study or other school duties."[7]

Students were free to take part in any recreational activities they wished to from 4:30 to 6:00. Supper was served at 6:00 p.m.—"evening devotions being held just before the meal." Two and a half hours, from 7:00 to 9:30 were allocated for evening study, followed by a half hour of evening "silent time"—the taking of a few moments to close the day with prayer and/or the reading of Scripture. "Lights out" came at 10:00, whereupon a student "floor officer" would walk the hall to make sure no midnight oil would be burnt or hi-jinks clandestinely pursued.[8]

As for the school calendar, Mount Hermon remained in continuous session, the year being divided into three terms of four months each. Under this system the school facilities could be used in the summer, when expenses were at a minimum.[9]

During these early years, flexibility was the order of the day in terms of student instruction, which was "adapted in an extraordinary degree to the individual needs of the pupil." Those who had received a solid early education were prepared for college, or given "a thorough course in English branches, adding in each case a course in Bible study." At the same time, older students who had been deprived of early educational advantages and who might have possessed "a larger knowledge of life and wider acquaintance with the Scriptures" wrestled with acquiring the rudiments of the education they had not received in their younger years. Seated at a table by lantern light, these boys might be seen learning the multiplication table, or trying "with knitted brows to master the grammatical structure of simple sentences."[10]

Aside from helping boys with varied backgrounds receive instruction in areas where their education might have been deficient prior to entering Mount Hermon, more formal and structured approaches to study were available as well. The preparatory course provided instruction in "the elementary branches." The classical course, four years in length, gave "adequate preparation for admission to any college." Many students who undertook the classical course were later admitted to many well-known colleges. Meanwhile, the scientific course "afforded preparation for the best schools of technology, or secured a good practical education" for those who would not be going on to college. Lastly, the elective course was offered "to those whose circumstances demand more freedom in the choice of studies than the other courses allow."[11]

Memorial Chapel was the center of spiritual life at Mount Hermon. And while something more of the spiritual environment fostered at the school shall be said in a moment, the story associated with the creation of Memorial Chapel is one that should be recounted.

When Memorial Chapel was built, it was situated, as Will Moody wrote, "upon a prominence that [Father] playfully called 'Temptation Hill'—hinting that some friend might be tempted to give the money necessary to erect a chapel. But as the hint had not been taken, the sixtieth anniversary of his birthday in 1897 was made the occasion of an effort to provide this much-needed building." It was a most welcome event— one that Will remembered gave his father "as much happiness as any present made to him personally. Accordingly, the funds necessary were raised in England and America by the voluntary contributions of friends who wished to share in this tribute of love and gratitude. The Rev. F. B. Meyer, of London, and H. M. Moore, of Boston, were responsible for this suggestion and its consummation."[12]

When completed, Memorial Chapel seated one thousand people. And although it was built expressly as a memorial of Moody's sixtieth birthday, he would not, Will wrote, "allow this fact to be mentioned on the bronze tablet in the vestibule." Such a gesture was entirely in keeping with Moody's character. Thus the bronze tablet read: "This chapel was erected by the united contributions of Christian friends in Great Britain and the United States, for the glory of God and to be a perpetual witness to their unity in the service of Christ."[13]

≈

"Unity in the service of Christ" was a watchword for all that Moody cherished in his hopes for the Mount Hermon School (and the Northfield Seminary). Will Moody was witness to this firsthand and, as he recalled, "In both [of the] Northfield schools, the end in view [was] to impart knowledge, not so much as an accomplishment [in and of itself,] but as a means of making men and women more serviceable to society."[14]

In short, the gifts and talents each student possessed were to be carefully cultivated and nurtured—that in the future these young men and women would enter spheres of service fully recognizing they were among those "to whom much had been given."[15] It was devoutly hoped that their lives and future endeavors would henceforth be guided by the desire to make a grateful return in service to God and others for all they had been given. It was a noble vision—one born of the hardscrabble experiences out of which God had called D. L. Moody himself. The life he now knew was far beyond anything he could have asked or imagined for himself as a fatherless boy raised in poverty. He had not had any of the opportunities he now cherished for the young men and women attending the Northfield schools; but he could impart them.

To foster this good end, the Christian faith was held forth for students as the source of every gift or talent that students might possess. Gifts and talents were blessings bestowed by a gifting God—a Savior Moody wished them all to know and love as he did. And so, every course of study at the Northfield schools included what was then called "Bible training." By 1900, eight hundred students at the Northfield Seminary and the Mount Hermon School were receiving instruction in the Scriptures twice a week.[16]

Will Moody described the results that flowed from this: "In the twenty years that have elapsed since these two schools were first established, nearly six thousand students have felt the influence of the work, and hundreds have given their time and talent to the proclamation of the Gospel they heard at Northfield. Others have entered various occupations, where their quiet influence is doubtless felt at home or in business.[17]

The spirit of the Mount Hermon School, as the Reverend Alexander McGaffin of Brooklyn wrote, could be captured in a homely phrase: *hermonology*. He described what his life at the school was like in an extended series of reflections. "I went to Mount Hermon," he remembered, "as a mere boy—without any particular aim in life or any serious religious convictions. There I came upon a species of Christianity altogether new to me . . . an educational training tempered by an earnest religious spirit. One did not study merely for learning's sake, nor was one religious merely for religion's sake. A great purpose was constantly held up, towards which we were . . . to struggle."[18]

What was that purpose? McGaffin expressed it this way: "We were taught that the present was the means and the future the end; that in that future dwelt God and humanity, and that our work would have to do with them."[19]

McGaffin then came to the heart of what he remembered, and it was here that his recollections took on a lyrical quality.

Following is a recollection of what he and his fellow students were taught:

> [T]he great need of the Eternal One was the cry of His heart for the world; and the great need of man was his undefined longing for God.
>
> The italicised words in the vocabulary of God, we were taught, are "the world" and "redemption." There is a divine voice, they told us at Mount Hermon, a divine voice speaking, in divine language from Heaven, a message to man, and a human voice speaking in human language, disconnected and wandering, uttering . . . the cravings of the soul.
>
> We were to be mediators who could hear the voice from Heaven, could understand the divine language, and could repeat the message over again in words that man might catch, in tones that would reach his heart.
>
> This was to be the practical religion and constant duty of every one of us, whatever our avocation in the world . . . This is a sublime mission in the world, and one which was constantly presented to us at Mount Hermon. All our training, educational and religious, was intended to fit us for this work . . .
>
> Of the men whom I know to be in darkness and doubt today the majority of them are those who never have been rightly instructed, or who have never seen the religion of Jesus rightly lived. No one can have been a student at Mount Hermon and have missed either. I speak feelingly and I speak with knowledge. Mount Hermon was the gateway of Heaven for me . . . It helped me to cherish every lofty desire. It inspired

me with courage . . . It placed before me a holy ambition, and when it launched my little craft out into deep water, there were a compass and pilot aboard—and I have not yet run aground.[20]

McGaffin wrote of the spiritual life and environment he knew during his years at Mount Hermon. But there was another aspect of his time that lingered in his memory as well. He set great store on the educational value of Mount Hermon. "It is certainly unique," he recalled. "After seven years' study since leaving the school, I can sincerely say that the best teacher I have ever had was she with whom I began my studies in Greek. For thoroughness, painstaking care, and inspiration, I have never met her equal. Her teaching, like that of all the others, was characterized by an earnestness of purpose and purity of motive which I have seen in only a few instances since."[21]

Instruction in the Christian life and Scriptures lay at the heart of Mount Hermon's institutional life (as it did at the Northfield Seminary); but amidst this spiritual climate, academic rigor and excellence flourished. McGaffin drew attention to this:

Teaching was regarded at Mount Hermon as a sacred privilege, and was pursued in that spirit . . . More good students are made at Mount Hermon than at most institutions of secondary education. It was not a matter of surprise to those who knew the school, though it was astonishing to some who did not know it, that two of its graduates were the only members of a freshman class in one of the three great colleges of the

East who were first honor men in every subject . . . Two of our men from the same class at [Mount] Hermon have been valedictorians of their respective classes at college, while a third was the holder of the historical fellowship at another university. These are a few instances of winning work of which I have personal knowledge; there are many others.[22]

It would have rejoiced D. L. Moody's heart to read McGaffin's words, which were published a year after his death in 1899. But then, he had seen for many years how young men and women like McGaffin had flourished amidst the atmosphere of faith and learning that had taken root at Northfield and Mount Hermon. It was a goodly sight.

THE BIBLE INSTITUTE

Even though Chicago was no longer Moody's home, it was never far from his mind. In 1886 he decided to do something for Chicago—the city that lay close to his heart. He would establish a school for the nations in the heart of the city.

Such a goal had long been a dream and ministry aspiration for a remarkable woman whom Moody knew well and highly respected: Miss Emma Dryer. For years she had cherished a vision for such a place. Yet a problem presented itself. She and her Chicago-based coworkers could be the hands and feet of such an enterprise, but they needed a prominent guiding spirit and fund-raiser to make it happen. They knew that Moody was just the man to help them realize this dream.

Before the story of how this dream unfolded can be told, however, more should be said about Emma Dryer—and there is good reason why. For it is not too much to say that D. L. Moody's interest in educational philanthropy took root in the summer of 1870, when he met Emma Dryer, a principal and teacher at Illinois State Normal University.[1]

Just two years older than Moody, Emma Dryer had also suffered crushing loss as a child. Where Moody had lost his father at age four, both of Emma Dryer's parents died when she was yet a child herself. Raised by an aunt who could afford to give her a fine education, Emma thrived from elementary school onward. She graduated with highest honors from LeRoy Female Seminary, and soon afterward joined the faculty of Knoxville Female College in Tennessee. Leaving this school during the Civil War, she joined the faculty of Illinois State Normal University in 1864. During her summers and holidays, she busied herself in Christian ministry, teaching the less fortunate, sharing her faith with them, and serving alongside friends in relief work to aid people in need.[2]

Then, in 1870, everything changed. Emma contracted typhoid fever and became deathly ill. No one expected her to live. But, as she and her friends believed ever after, God wrought a miracle in her life and she experienced a complete healing. In the days following her astonishing recovery, she could only think that God, in His grace and mercy, had spared her life for a great purpose. She resolved henceforth to minister to "the needs of the dying world, as never before."[3]

Resigning her position as head of the women's faculty at Illinois State Normal University, she moved to Chicago, not knowing (at age thirty-five) precisely what the future held for her. What she lost in terms of a good salary, and the place of respect and security she had known at the university, was more than compensated for when she met Dwight and Emma Moody and the W. H. Daniels family soon after her arrival in Chicago.[4]

As Lyle W. Dorsett has observed, D. L. Moody "could not help but admire a woman who had shown so much courage in forsaking all she had known to devote herself fully to relief work. He had wrestled with the same decision in 1860, leaving his business career at the height of his success."[5]

Moody and Dryer soon united in what the reformer William Wilberforce once called "concerts of benevolence."[6] At Moody's urging, Emma took on two new roles: head of the Chicago Women's Aid Society and superintendent of the Women's Auxiliary of the YMCA (a forerunner of the YWCA).

Creative, tireless, and able, Emma served superbly in these roles. So it was not surprising that early in 1873, on the eve of departing for his first great preaching campaign in Britain, Moody had persuaded her to take the leading role in yet another new venture: the foundation of a school to train women, and eventually men as well, in preparation for service in home or foreign missions or evangelistic work. It would be a school that would provide systematic training of the Bible, theology, and practical ministry.[7]

By 1877, W. H. Daniels had taken to calling this school "Mr. Moody's Theological Seminary." This was intended as a kindness and a recognition of Moody's indispensable role as the major fund-raiser for the school. But it should always be remembered that it was Emma Dryer who took those funds—bringing her gifts for administration, innovation, curriculum development, and leadership to bear—and made this school a reality. D. L. Moody and Emma Dryer were a team, and the shared memory of what they did in these years should be handed down to posterity.[8]

Records for one year during the first years of "Mr. Moody's Seminary" have survived. What they reveal is impressive. Under Emma Dryer's supervision, 673 cottage prayer meetings were held, 479 visits to the sick were undertaken, and 10,628 tracts and religious papers were distributed. Meetings of various kinds abounded—all with a view to providing a support network for families or to teach a handicraft. Seventy-eight mothers' meetings were held; there were 502 sessions of "sewing-schools" and 165 school prayer-meetings. Regular hours for Bible study were also a daily fixture.[9]

Such success led Emma Dryer to urge Moody at every opportunity to start a training school for young men and women.[10] She could see that from such humble beginnings, the school she had started could become more than it then was.

≈

Early in 1883, several Chicago-based friends began meeting weekly with Emma Dryer to pray that D. L. Moody would return to Chicago and help them develop their new school more fully. Still, their weekly meetings remained just that for some three years. It was not until January 22, 1886—when a meeting in Chicago to discuss city evangelization was held—that the subject of a training school was taken up in earnest.[11]

When Moody rose to address this gathering, his words left little doubt that Emma Dryer's years of consistent encouragement and urging about the Chicago school were uppermost in his thoughts. "I tell you what I want," he said, "and what I have on my heart. I believe we have got to have gap-men to stand between the laity and the ministers; men who are trained to do city mission work. Take men that have the gifts and train them for the work of reaching the people."

So it was that the Chicago Evangelization Society, later renamed the Moody Bible Institute, was born.[12] Its mission statement was a realization of Emma Dryer's hopes and D. L. Moody's vision. It would foster the "education and training of Christian workers, including teachers, ministers, missionaries . . . who may completely and effectively proclaim the gospel of Jesus Christ."[13] One hundred and twenty-three years on, the Moody Bible Institute (MBI) endures and continues its commitment to this mission.

Young men and women from every corner of the globe can now receive a first-rate education in the heart of America's second city. Undergraduates can pursue a diverse array of studies, including biblical languages, communications, electronic media, youth ministry, pastoral studies, women's ministries, sacred music, theology, apologetics, world missions and evangelism, urban ministries, and applied linguistics. Graduate students can earn advanced degrees in biblical studies, intercultural studies, urban studies and spiritual formation, as well as the more traditional master of divinity. Were Emma Dryer and D. L. Moody to see MBI now, it would be more than they could have asked or imagined.

GOD'S HERALD IN THE GILDED AGE

Whenever [Mr. Moody] told a story, or related a personal experience, it was invariably to illustrate a great and living truth.[1]

—C. F. Goss

This is the preacher who cracked open the skies for thousands and let the unearthly light come through.

—R. P. T. Coffin

Dwight Moody was part of the wide world of my boyhood,"[2] Pulitzer Prize–winning poet Robert P. Tristram Coffin wrote in May 1938. So began a remarkable review of *My Father: An Intimate Portrait of Dwight Moody*, by his son Paul D. Moody, then president of Middlebury College, and published by the distinguished house of Little,

Brown and Company. Coffin's article was as much retrospective as review, and it describes many of the reasons why D. L. Moody captured and held an enduring place in the popular imagination of the late nineteenth and early twentieth century.

Coffin was born in 1892, some seven years before the evangelist's death; and it seems that well before he learned anything about the wider world beyond his home in coastal Maine, D. L. Moody was a person he'd come to know well.

His name was on a book that spelt holiness and rest and music to me. I ranked the book level with "Pilgrim's Progress" and the one with Doré's illustrations of *Paradise Lost*. It was the book of Gospel hymns, and it was kept on the melodeon in the parlor of our farmhouse. Moody and Sankey were a part of my Mondays and Tuesdays, too, as well as Sundays, because my father was always singing Moody and Sankey hymns while he worked. My father was a man built big, and he worked hard and sang hard and beautiful when he was working. To this day, I cannot hear boards being sawn without hearing [the hymn] "Hold the Fort."[3]

> *Fierce and long the battle rages, but our help is near;*
> *Onward comes our great Commander, cheer,*
> *my comrades, cheer!*
> *"Hold the fort, for I am coming," Jesus signals still;*
> *Wave the answer back to Heaven, "By Thy grace we will."*

"I might have guessed," Coffin continued, "that the man on the hymnbook cover was like my father. Now his son's book tells me he was. The evangelist we entertained on our farm was a man built big like my father and took up more than his share of the carriage seat. A big man . . . big in his mind just the same as everywhere else. And full of the grace of being a human being."[4]

Calling Moody "the Yankee Gidjon," a phrase meant to convey the image of a spiritual bard in homespun, Coffin commenced his retrospective with a one-sentence phrase: "I want faith's got legs 'n c'n run round." This, he affirmed, "is a good portrait of the man himself. Dwight Moody ran around. He ran around over our country and England, and other places, for many years. He got around spry, in spite of his being built like Sir John Falstaff."[5]

Coffin's reference to Moody's ability to turn a colorful phrase highlights an important reason for Moody's popular appeal—his gift for communicating spiritual truth in a way that was winsome and accessible. Billy Graham, it has been said, always sought "to put the cookies on the lower shelf" when preaching—that is, he spoke in ways readily understood, even by those who were unchurched. Long years before, Moody had begun weaving the rustic proverbs he learned as a boy into his sermons. Over time, he took to coining phrases of his own with the ease of a born raconteur. Both were techniques that came naturally to him, and are reminiscent of the gilded age's most celebrated speaker, Mark Twain. In saying "I want faith's got legs 'n c'n run round," Moody was—in an understated, memorable way—making an important point about the connection between faith and the good works that ought to flow naturally from it.

This was a colorful, rather easygoing admonition; but at other times Moody could be bracing in his use of word pictures, as in this challenge to the cold and lifeless conformity that characterized so much nineteenth-century spirituality—a recurring theme of his preaching: "There are too many religious meetings which are sadder than a funeral. They are hindrance to the cause. They breed people with faces bearing an expression as chilling as an east blast from the lake."[6]

One trait Coffin particularly admired was Moody's unconventionality:

> Dwight Moody's fondness for speed showed in his prayers. He made them short. He won his greatest convert by stopping a long-winded prayer. It was in London. "While our brother is finishing his prayer," he rose and said, "let us sing hymn number so and so."
>
> So an indifferent young Englishman turned his face west, found him an icy empire to heal bodies and minds in, won a knighthood the best possible way, and wrote his name forever on Labrador [the Canadian province close to my home in Maine]. It was Wilfred Grenfell [the great medical missionary and benefactor].[7]

Coffin also discerned in Moody a man of hidden depths, a "philosopher of goodness" often revealed in a simply wrought but telling phrase—such as Moody's definition of character as "what a man is in the dark."[8]

Saying that his fellow New Englander was "a power for

good in the whole world," Coffin closed his review with as a fine an endorsement of Moody as has ever been written. Coming as it did from an able and learned critic—a Rhodes Scholar as well as a Pulitzer Prize winner, it has added weight: "This," Coffin said, "is a good man to know."[9]

≈

Coffin's assessment, valuable though it is, does not give the whole picture of why Moody was such a well-regarded figure. There are other, no less important sides of who he was.

One harkens back to Moody's unconventionality as a speaker. Dry, censorious, turgid, and often brimstonish homilies were a staple of nineteenth-century preaching and a reason why many stayed away from church. Moody's sermons were nothing like this, and they stood out.

Because he was never ordained and had no formal training for the ministry, Moody never became steeped in the hoary traditions of a church that in many respects had become stagnant with them.[10] Using Christ's parables as a model, he interspersed his sermons repeatedly with stories. "Men will listen to a story," he said, "when they won't listen to Scripture, and the moral of a story remains with them a long time, and often sets them thinking along the lines they refuse to consider in sermon form."[11] One recollection shows how effective a device Moody's use of stories could be:

I [Moody] remember, when a boy upon a farm in New England, [a family] had a well, and they put in an old wooden pump, and I used to have to pump the water from that well upon wash-day, and to water the cattle; and I had to pump and pump and pump until my arm got tired, many a time.

But they have a better way now; they don't dig down a few feet and brick up the hole and put the pump in, but they go down through the clay and the sand and the rock, and on down until they strike what they call a lower stream, and then it becomes an artesian well, which needs no labor, as the water rises spontaneously from the depths beneath. Now I think God wants all His children to be a sort of artesian well; not to keep pumping, but to flow right out.[12]

A. T. Pierson—a graduate of the prestigious Union Theological seminary in New York, and Charles Spurgeon's successor in the pulpit of the Metropolitan Tabernacle of London—penned what is still one of the best descriptions of Moody's preaching style: "[Mr. Moody] had learned to preach simply—let us rather say he had not learned to preach other- wise; and in the unaffected language of nature, uncorrupted by the fastidious nature of the schools, he spoke face to face with men; and they heard him. Sprightly and vivacious, with a touch of humor as well as pathos, [he was] direct and pointed in his appeals . . ."[13]

For his part, Lord Shaftesbury, the greatest social reformer of the age, once thanked God publicly that Moody had not been educated at Oxford, "for he had a wonderful power of getting at the hearts of men, and while the common people hear him gladly, many persons of high station have been greatly struck with the marvelous simplicity and power of his preaching." [To this] Lord Shaftesbury added that the Lord Chancellor of England a short time before had said to him, "The simplicity of that man's preaching, the clear manner in which he sets forth salvation by Christ, is to me the most striking and the most delightful thing I ever knew in my life."[14]

Storytelling is a staple of preaching now. But in Moody's time, it was a novel and appealing innovation, especially in the extent to which he used it. And the proof was in the response— hundreds of thousands heeded his call to embrace the Christian faith. Humor, pathos, local color—all were arrows in Moody's metaphorical quiver. He used them often and with great success. As his friend C. F. Goss recalled:

> [Mr. Moody's] illustrations were always of the simplest possible character and abounded largely in personal reminiscences. They were sometimes classical, for he had listened to so many eloquent speakers that striking stories from antiquity became familiar to him without his having to discover them through reading.
>
> There were a few scientific ones which he acquired from the same source, and occasional tropes and metaphors indicated that he had observed natural analogies.
>
> But in the main his illustrations were narratives of real life. As he told the story of Noah's warnings before the Flood, he pictured the scoffers of that day while the Deluge was delayed.
>
> "They'd say to one another, 'Not much sign of old

Noah's rainstorm yet.' They'd talk it over in the corner groceries, evenings."

Then, as if in explanation, he added:

"I tell you, my friends, before the world got as bad as it
was in Noah's day, they must have had corner groceries."[15]

In this way, Moody was more like Twain than many of his
preaching peers and contemporaries. He was more a raconteur
than a railer, or rhetorician. And lest there were those who were
inclined to censure what they considered simplistic preaching,
he defended the practice: "Many and many a time I have found
that when the sermon—and even the text—has been forgotten, some story has fastened itself in a hearer's mind, and has
borne fruit. *Anecdotes are like windows to let light in upon a subject.* They have a useful ministry."[16]

Open as Moody was to innovation, his sermons did
typically have a certain, albeit simple, structure. He would commence with a brief statement of his central point, such as "God
supplies us with just as much grace as we need." He would then
introduce a relevant passage of Scripture, followed by a story,
or perhaps two, to illustrate the central point or a spiritual truth.
One memorable vignette concerned a woman he called Lady
Pendulum:

God supplies us with just as much grace as we need, and no
more. Don't be afraid you won't get all you require. I was
once talking with an English woman on this subject. She was
afraid she couldn't live a Christian life, because there would

be so many trials and temptations in future. I tried in one way and another to convince her that she need have no misgivings—that God would supply daily grace sufficient for every emergency.

Nothing availed till I used the old story of the clock. The pendulum of a clock once became discouraged—didn't see how it was ever going to tick out all the hours it was expected to measure. The clock reasoned with it, saying, "Only one tick at a time," and so it went on with its slow and steady "tick-tick." The lady caught the idea, and talked so much about that clock that people called her Lady Pendulum. She sent me a beautiful clock, that's now ticking away over at my house.[17]

Moody would then conclude with a concise restatement of his original point—in this case: "The Lord will always give us grace as we ask for it."

Over the course of a sermon, Moody might repeat this basic pattern two or three times—constructing, by the time he had finished speaking, what has now come to be known as the classic three-point sermon. He would then close with a plea for his hearers to place their faith in Christ.

⌐

Music played an indispensable part in Moody's preaching. And if Billy Graham had George Beverly Shea, Moody was blessed some seventy years earlier with Ira Sankey, whose rich baritone voice and gifts as a keyboardist meant that the hymns used in preaching tours could come to life through instantly singable melodies and a heartfelt, often moving lyric—such as Elizabeth Clephane's rendering of Christ's parable of the lost sheep:

> There were ninety and nine that safely lay
> In the shelter of the fold.
> But one was out on the hills away,
> Far off from the gates of gold.
> Away on the mountains wild and bare.
> Away from the tender Shepherd's care.
> Away from the tender Shepherd's care.
> "Lord, Thou hast here Thy ninety and nine;
> Are they not enough for Thee?"
> But the Shepherd made answer: "This of Mine
> Has wandered away from Me;
> And although the road be rough and steep,
> I go to the desert to find My sheep,
> I go to the desert to find My sheep."

It was an elegantly simple and effective format. People left the venues where Moody preached with a hymn or a story (or both) that would linger in their heart and memory.

Moody often displayed a cheerful willingness to change things up in the course of a sermon. "Let's have that hymn again," he would say. The idea was to repeat the hymn a few times "until all were familiar with it, and could sing it in a spirited manner."[18] Of such a practice Moody was wont to say:

I wish we had more liberty in our churches, so that when we had a subject, we could take a new hymn and practice it over and over again till we all knew it. You didn't know that hymn [we sang] before, but you caught it up in five minutes. A great many people would be shocked if we did that in a church service, but it is worthwhile to spend five minutes that way now and then, in the regular service. It is the only time you can get the people together. We want to break up these forms, and during the service if the subject suggests a new hymn, just teach it to the people right on the spot, and send them away with it ringing in their minds.[19]

"What we need," he concluded, "is singing that will bring out the gospel in such shape that the people won't forget it . . . Do you get good music? Get the young people to sing, and in that way you will waken up a fresh interest."[20]

This was Moody at his most compellingly unconventional and subversive, and it is worth noting that in this he and Sankey anticipated—by the better part of one hundred years—the atmosphere of praise songs being sung several times through to foster a spirit of worship and bring a moving message home to the heart.

≈

At his best, Moody displayed a genius—one might call it an artistry—for metaphor that was simply wrought, but deeply stirring. Some artists display a natural skill in oils. Moody was a naturally gifted painter of word pictures.

This presents a counterpoint to Robert Coffin's conception of Moody as "the Yankee Gidjon." To be sure, that was one side of him—the rustic spiritual bard with a ready supply of colorful sayings. It endeared him to many. But there were other, more subtle and profound sides too.

This can be seen in his gift for a one-sentence summary of the gospel, as in his phrase: "There is no man so far gone, but the grace of God can reach him."[21]

At other times he could, within the space of a paragraph, expound memorably on a passage of Scripture. For example: "'The Son of Man is come to seek and to save that which was lost.'—Luke 19:10. To me this is one of the sweetest verses in the whole Bible. In this one little short sentence we are told what Christ came into this world for. He came for a purpose; He came to do a work, and in this little verse the whole story is told. He came not to condemn the world, but that the world, through Him, might be saved."[22]

Then there were occasions when Moody's reflections possessed a vivid, sometimes beautiful imagery, as in the following two instances:

> The very first thing that happened after the news reached heaven of the fall of man, was that God came straight down to seek out the lost one. As He walks through the garden in the cool of the day, you can hear him calling "Adam! Adam! *Where are thou?*" It was the voice of grace, of mercy, and of love.[23]
>
> The world is in darkness, and the gospel offers light. Because man will not believe the gospel that Christ is the light

of the world, the world is dark to-day. But the moment a man believes, the light from Calvary crosses his path and he walks in an unclouded sun.[24]

Finally, there were times when Moody's extended reflections reached a very high level of preaching. One instance concerns how the words of the gospel removed his once pervasive fear of death. "I want to tell you why I like the gospel," he began:

It is because it has been the very best news I have ever heard. That is just why I like to preach it, because it has done me so much good. No man can ever tell what it has done for him, but I think I can tell what it has *undone*.

It has taken out of my path four of the bitterest enemies I ever had. There is that terrible enemy mentioned in First Corinthians Chapter 15, the last enemy, Death. The gospel has taken it out of the way.

My mind very often rolls back twenty years ago, before I was converted, and I think how dark it used to seem, as I thought of the future. I well remember how I used to look on death as a terrible monster, how he used to throw his dark shadow across my path; how I trembled as I thought of the terrible hour when he should come for me . . .

It was the custom in our village to toll from the old church bell the age of any one who died. Death never entered that village and tore away one of the inhabitants but I counted the tolling of the bell. Sometimes it was seventy, sometimes eighty, sometimes it would be away down among the teens, sometimes it would toll out the death of some one of my own age. It made a solemn impression upon me . . . I thought of the cold hand of death feeling for the cords of life. I thought of being launched forth to spend my eternity in an unknown land . . .

But that is all changed now. The grave has lost its terror. As I go on towards heaven I can shout, "O death! Where is thy sting?" and I hear the answer rolling down from Calvary—"buried in the bosom of the Son of God." He took the sting right out of death for me, and received it into his own bosom. . . . That last enemy has been overcome, and I can look on death as a crushed victim. All that death can get now is this old [body], and I do not care how quickly I get rid of it. I shall get a glorified body, a resurrection body, a body much better than this.

Suppose death should come stealing up into this pulpit, and lay his icy hand upon my heart, and it should cease to throb. I should rise to the better world to be present with the King. The gospel has made an enemy a friend. What a glorious thought, that when you die you but sink into the arms of Jesus, to be borne to the land of everlasting rest![25]

Perhaps the best and most moving instance of Moody's preaching concerns his eyewitness account of an event that took place near the close of the Civil War. What he saw then helped him understand the release of the Christian from the chains of sin and death in a new and utterly unforgettable way:

It was my privilege to go into Richmond with General Grant's army. I had not been long there before it was announced that the negroes were going to have a jubilee meeting. These coloured people were just coming into liberty; their chains were falling off, and they were just awakening to the fact that they were free.

I thought it would be a great event, and I went down to the African Church, one of the largest in the South, and found it crowded. One of the coloured chaplains of a northern regiment had offered to speak.

I have heard many eloquent men in Europe and in America, but I do not think I ever heard eloquence such as I heard that day. He said, "Mothers! you rejoice to-day; you are for ever free! That little child has been torn from your embrace, and sold off to some distant state for the last time. Your hearts are never to be broken again in that way; you are free!"

The women clapped their hands and shouted at the top of their voices, "Glory, glory to God!" It was good news to them, and they believed it. It filled them full of joy.

Then [the chaplain] turned to the young men, and said, "Young men! you rejoice to-day; you have heard the crack of the slave-driver's whip for the last time—your posterity shall be free! young men rejoice to-day, you are for ever free!" And they clapped their hands, and shouted, "Glory to God!" They believed the good tidings.

"Young maidens!" he said [last of all], "you rejoice to-day. You have been put on the auction-block and sold for the last time; you are free—for ever free!" They believed it, and lifting up their voices, shouted, "Glory be to God!" I never was in such a meeting.[26]

≈

Not long after Moody's death, the *New York Times* hailed him as a man who "did more to convert people to the profession of the Christian faith than any clergyman of his time."[27] Still, the *Times* noted, "Moody was a New Englander of a common type. Thousands of Massachusetts farmers and merchants have looked like him, talked like him, lived much as he lived. [The] special gift that distinguished him among his fellows was . . . personal magnetism."[28]

The anonymous reviewer for the *Times* was right so far as he went, but left a good deal unsaid. All that Moody brought to his preaching was cultivated in a seed-bed of faith. His experience, personality, and gifts—all these were nurtured through a confluence of spiritual streams. What shone through as a result has been well described by scholar Michael Tatem: "Moody's . . . warmth and compassion for the people to whom he ministered is made apparent in his stories and illustrations. The honesty, sincerity, humility, and enthusiasm reflected in his sermons give reason enough for Moody's appeal to the masses."[29]

This, under the blessing of God, is what set Moody apart.

"THE VERY JAWS
OF DEATH"

For it is thou, Lord, thou Lord only, that makest me
dwell in safety.

—Samuel Wesley, a paraphrase of Psalm 4:8

On Wednesday, December 4, 1892, one of the most
harrowing episodes in D. L. Moody's life became front-
page news in the *New York Times*.[1]

No one could have foreseen why. In the autumn of 1892,
Moody and his family were in England, where one of his
preaching tours was drawing to a close. Not slated to end until
mid-November, D. L. had bid farewell several weeks earlier to
Emma and all of their children, except Will—who was con-
cluding a course of graduate study in Germany. When Will had
finished, the plan was for father and son to meet and take ship
from Southampton. Both looked forward to a leisurely cruise

home, where they could make up for lost time and enjoy each other's company.[2]

"My last day in London," Moody recalled, "was a pleasant one; a day of promise it might have been called, for the sun shone out brightly after some of those dark, foggy days so common in London. A company of friends gathered at the station to see me off."[3]

The thought of a restful return home was more than a welcome prospect. Just before embarking, Moody had thought it necessary to consult a noted physician. Worrisome symptoms had developed, and he wanted to know what might be wrong. As he wrote: "I called upon a celebrated physician, who told me that my heart was weakening and that I had to let up on my work, that I had to be more careful of myself . . . I was going home with the thought that I would not work quite so hard."[4]

The Moodys and the 750 other passengers on board the German steamer *Spree* were three days and eleven hundred miles out into the Atlantic when, in the early morning hours of Saturday, November 27, the main shaft of the ship's propeller broke. The next few moments were fixed indelibly in Moody's memory:

> Suddenly I was startled by a terrible crash and shock, as if the vessel had been driven on a rock. I did not at first feel much anxiety—perhaps I was too ill [from seasickness due to a rough sea] to think about it.
>
> My son jumped from his berth, and rushed on deck. He was back again in a few moments, saying that the shaft was broken and the vessel [was] sinking.

I did not at first believe it could be so bad, but concluded to dress and go on deck. The report was only too true. The captain told the affrighted passengers, who had rushed on deck, that there was no danger, and some of the second-cabin passengers returned to their berths, only to be driven out again by the in-rushing water, leaving everything behind them.

The officers and crew did all they could to save the vessel. But it was soon found that the pumps were useless, for the water poured into the ship too rapidly to be controlled. There was nothing more . . . to do. We were utterly, absolutely helpless.[5]

The force of the propeller shear had been terrific, so much so that two large pieces of it were blown through the bottom of the ship.[6] "The gloom and terror that followed the accident cannot easily be described,"[7] wrote General Oliver Otis Howard, a friend of Moody's who had also booked passage on the *Spree*. Almost immediately, electrical power was lost. The ship and her terrified passengers were plunged into darkness, even as the crew scrambled to close her watertight compartments.

In whatever way they could, passengers made their way to the ship's top deck as quickly as possible. Yet there was little else for them to do but huddle together in the darkness, not knowing what fate awaited them. Moody, like everyone else, feared the worst. The scene that met his eyes was one of barely controlled panic:

We could only stand still on the poor, drifting, sinking ship and look into our watery graves. All this time, unknown to the passengers, the officers were making preparations for the last resort. The lifeboats were all put in readiness, provisions prepared, life-preservers in hand, the officers armed with revolvers to enforce their orders . . . The question was evidently being debated in their mind whether to launch the boats at once, or wait. [But] the sea was so heavy that the boats could hardly live in it. Two of the passengers had loaded revolvers ready to blow out their brains if the vessel should go down, preferring death by bullet to death by drowning.[8]

By noon on Saturday the captain of the *Spree* believed the flow of water into the crippled ship was under control and expressed the hope that she might drift "in the way of some passing vessel." Still, as the hours passed, no vessel appeared on the horizon. Moody recalled what he and everyone else felt:

The ship's bow was now high in the air, while the stern seemed to settle more and more. The sea was very rough, and the ship rolled from side to side with fearful lurches. If she had pitched violently but once, the bulkheads must have burst, and the end come.

The captain tried to keep up hope by telling us we should probably drift in the way of a ship by three o'clock that . . . afternoon, but the night closed upon us without a sign of a sail. That was an awful night, the darkest in all our lives!

Seven hundred men, women, and children waiting for the doom that was settling upon us! No one dared to sleep . . .

Sunday morning dawned without help or hope. Up to that time no suggestion of religious services had been made. To have done that would almost certainly have produced a panic. In the awful suspense and dread that prevailed, a word about religion would have suggested the most terrible things to the passengers. But [a little later on Sunday morning], I asked General O. O. Howard, who was with us, to secure the captain's permission for a service in the [dining salon].[9]

There are times when a point of crisis brings out the best in people. Despite the gnawing fear that gripped Moody, God granted him a measure of strength and fortitude that began to sustain him. In whatever time he had left, he resolved to do what he could to prepare himself and his fellow passengers for eternity.

General Howard readily agreed with Moody's suggestion about a service and went in search of the captain. He found the beleaguered man "suffering excruciatingly" in his cabin from an attack of gallstones. He was having to direct the gallant efforts of his crew from a bed of pain. Still, he readily assented to General Howard's request, likely thinking that aside from any religious comfort, it would at least give his overwrought passengers something to do.

And so a service was arranged between ten and eleven o'clock that morning in the dining salon. Howard then reported back to Moody. "Tell the people," he said. Whereupon General Howard went one way and Will Moody the other, spreading the word.[10]

"To our surprise," Moody later said, "nearly every passenger attended."[11] So began a service filled with a greater sense of urgency than any other in his life. As he recalled, it was not easily done:

> With one arm clasping a pillar to steady myself on the reeling vessel, I tried to read the ninety-first Psalm, and we prayed that God would still the raging of the sea and bring us to our desired haven.
>
> It was a new psalm to me from that hour. The eleventh verse touched me very deeply. It was like a voice of divine assurance, and it seemed a very real thing as I read: "He shall give His angels charge over thee, to keep thee in all thy ways."
>
> Surely He did it. I read also from Psalm 107:20–31.
>
> One lady thought those words must have been written for the occasion, and afterward asked to see the Bible for herself. A German translated verse by verse as I read, for the benefit of his countrymen.
>
> I was passing through a new experience. I had thought myself superior to the fear of death. I had often preached on the subject, and urged Christians to realize this victory of faith.
>
> During the Civil War I had been under fire without fear. I was in Chicago during the great cholera epidemic, and went around with the doctors visiting the sick and dying. Where

they could go to look after the bodies of men I said I could go to look after their souls. I remember a case of small-pox where the flesh had literally dropped away from the backbone, yet I went to the bedside of that poor sufferer again and again, with Bible and prayer, for Jesus' sake.

In all this I had no fear of death. But on the sinking ship it was different. There was no cloud between my soul and my Savior. I knew my sins had been put away, and that if I died there it would be only to wake up in heaven. That was all settled long ago. But as my thoughts went out to my loved ones at home—my wife and children, my friends on both sides of the sea, the schools and all the interests so dear to me—and as I realized that perhaps the next hour would separate me forever from all these, so far as this world was concerned, I confess it almost broke me down.

It was the darkest hour of my life! I could not endure it. I must have relief, and relief came in prayer. God heard my cry, and enabled me to say, from the depth of my soul: "Thy will be done!" Sweet peace came to my heart.[12]

After the service, long hours passed. Evening came, with no sign of a ship approaching. But, as Moody remembered, "I went to bed and almost immediately fell asleep, and never slept more soundly in all my life."

At about three o'clock in the morning on Monday, November 29, Moody was aroused from a sound sleep by the voice of his son saying, "Come on deck, father." What followed is best told in Moody's own words:

I followed him, and he pointed to a far-off light, rising and sinking on the sea. It was a messenger of deliverance to us. It proved to be the light of the steamer *Lake Huron*, whose lookout had seen our flaming signals of distress, and supposed it was a vessel in flames.

Oh, the joy of that moment, when those seven hundred despairing passengers beheld the approaching ship! Who can ever forget it? But now the question was: Can this small steamer tow the helpless *Spree* a thousand miles to Queenstown [Ireland]? Every moment was watched with the [greatest] anxiety and prayer.

It was a brave and perilous undertaking. The two vessels were at last connected by two great cables. If a storm arose, these would snap like thread, and we must be left to our fate. But I had no fear. God would finish the work He had begun. The waves were calmed; the cables held; the steamer moved in the wake of the *Huron*. . . .

Seven days after the accident, by the good hand of our God upon us, we were able to hold a joyous thanksgiving service in the harbor of Queenstown. The rescuing ship that God sent to us in our distress had just sufficient power to tow our ship, and just enough coal to take her into port! Less would have been insufficient. Her captain also is a man of prayer, and he besought God's help to enable them to accomplish their dangerous and difficult task. God answered the united prayer of the distressed voyagers . . .

It had been little short of a miracle; and yet it was a miracle tempered by tragedy. Not all had escaped death, or the ravages of such a harrowing experience. Despite the deep and enduring gratitude that Moody and so many others felt, somber memories would always be with him:

> The nervous strain of those eight days and nights of suspense was something fearful. It was more than any one could long endure without help. The minds of several passengers gave way under the strain.
>
> A young Austrian, who had left his betrothed in Vienna, leaped overboard in despair, and was drowned before our eyes in spite of all we could do.
>
> It was a most pathetic sight to see a young mother, with two beautiful children, sitting in dumb anguish during the first forty-eight hours, never taking her eyes off her little ones; and if the ship had gone down, I have no doubt she would have gathered them to her bosom and gone down with them in her arms.
>
> There was a Russian Jew, who had taken passage without the knowledge of his relatives at home. It was pitiful to see his distress, as he confessed his sin, beat his breast, and denounced himself as the Jonah of the company. Kneeling upon the deck, with tears streaming down his cheeks, he cried to Jehovah not to visit the punishment of his sin upon all those unfortunate people.[13]

Joy colored D. L. and Will Moody's return to Northfield, where every building, it seemed, was illuminated to mark their arrival.[14] He never forgot the sight, nor would he ever lose a conviction that had settled firmly upon him. His life had been spared to some greater purpose. However much longer he might live, he would redeem the time given him with everything he had.

15

THINKING OUTSIDE THE BOX

Now I like the spirit in which our beloved friend and leader undertook this work. Some said, "Let us boycott the [World's] Fair;" others said, "Let us appeal to the law and put in money enough to prosecute its managers and compel them to shut it up." But our friend, Mr. Moody, said: "Now let us open so many preaching-places and present so many attractions that the people from all parts of the world will come and hear the gospel," and that is actually what has happened. . . . It is a remarkable movement.[1]

—A. J. Gordon

A typical enterprise of [Mr. Moody's] was the city-wide revival . . . in Chicago in 1893. Seizing the opportunity the Columbian Exposition of that year offered to win the ear of the whole world, he fairly took charge of the evangelistic life of the city for six months.[2]

—The New York Times

Many Christians in Chicago found reasons to disdain or militantly oppose the World's Colombian Exposition (or World's Fair) of 1893. They saw it was a den of lucre, if not iniquity—a Babylon to be shunned. That the fair would be open on Sunday was a particular source of irritation; and some wished to initiate legal proceedings to force it to close. Others openly called for a boycott.[3]

D. L. Moody was diametrically opposed to this. He saw the World's Fair as "the opportunity of a century"[4]—an insight that became a settled conviction when he was praying on the Mount of Olives in Israel during a visit there in the spring of 1892.[5] Chicago, the "second city" of America, was never far from his thoughts and heart. At this time, it was uppermost in his prayers.

That Chicago was America's second city was no overstatement. The census of 1890 revealed that for the first time, "Chicago was the second most populous city in the nation."[6] Not only was there a "vast unchurched population" in this Athens of the Midwest, but millions from every corner of America and the world were about to flock to her gates.

When Moody reflected on all this, he was in the city of David—where Christ had wept over that great city, saying: "O Jerusalem, Jerusalem . . . how often I have longed to gather your children together . . . but you were not willing."[7] One thought now etched itself in his mind. Were he to do nothing to reach these people, he could justly incur the reproach: "No man cares for my soul!"[8]

This conviction could not have been underscored more indelibly than when Moody had faced the prospect of death aboard the *Spree*. "When the announcement was made that the steamer was sinking," he recalled,

> and we were there in a helpless condition in mid-ocean, no one on earth knows what I passed through as I thought that my work was finished, and that I should never again have the privilege of preaching the Gospel of the Son of God. And on that dark night, the first night of the accident, I made a vow that if God would spare my life and bring me back to America, I would come to Chicago, and at the World's Fair preach the Gospel with all the power that He would give me.[9]

And so, his life spared, Moody returned to America to launch what would later be called "one of the greatest evangelistic crusades in Christian history."[10]

The Bible Institute of Chicago (founded just seven years before in 1886) became the headquarters for this outreach. To defray expenses, Moody was instrumental in raising monies equivalent to 1.2 million dollars in today's currency.[11] Auditoriums, theaters, halls, and tents were rented. Advertisements were created and given wide distribution. Speakers and singers were recruited, among them R. A. Torrey, A. J. Gordon, Thomas Spurgeon, and a gifted former baseball star for the Chicago White Stockings named Billy Sunday.

The services of preachers from Germany, Poland, Russia, France, and many Scandinavian countries were also retained. In a modern-day emulation of Pentecost, tens of thousands would thus be able to hear the gospel in their native language.

Songbooks were also printed in the major European languages: a prime example of which was the German edition of Ira Sankey's songs—translated and published by Walter Rauschenbusch, later so closely associated with the social gospel movement.[12] Lastly, a small army of 220 male and female students from the Bible Institute was marshaled to seize this historical moment in every conceivable way.[13] They fanned out into "churches, halls, auditoriums and tents all over downtown Chicago." Their charge: to preach and sing "the old Gospel [in] the power of the Holy Ghost."[14]

For six months in the summer of 1893, Moody and cohorts of volunteers did all they could to proclaim the good news. Near the Chicago stockyards, Moody himself rented Tattersalls, the huge arena that had so often been the venue for major political conventions and Wild West shows. As the campaign there commenced, Moody remarked: "We have got something better than Buffalo Bill, and we must get a bigger audience than he does."[15]

On a hot Sunday in June, early on in the fair's run, a Moody meeting drew an audience of 7,000—which half filled Tattersalls. At the same time, Moody steadfastly refused to censure the organizers of the fair for keeping its doors open on Sundays. Saying the gospel would prove stronger, his faith was rewarded in August when its organizers closed the fair on Sundays. Sunday after Sunday, attendance at the Moody meetings was exceeding 40,000, sometimes 50,000. Fair attendance had simultaneously suffered a precipitous decline. Its organizers realized there was little point in remaining open on Sundays when so many were going to hear Moody.[16]

In the end, an estimated 1,933,240 people—from every state and almost every nationality—attended events associated with the World's Fair Campaign.[17] It was, by any measure, a staggering success. Dr. Frederick Campbell expressed what many felt when he wrote: "[Mr. Moody] has once more proved himself to be a most remarkable instrument in the hands of Providence . . . If ordinary preachers had a little more of his audacity, with the faith and works which should accompany it, they would achieve greater things."[18]

At the close of the World's Fair in late October 1893, Moody was interviewed and asked to describe the results of the campaign he had initiated. He did so in the space of one compelling sentence. "Millions," he said, "have heard the simple Gospel preached by some of the most gifted preachers in the world; thousands have apparently been genuinely converted to Christ, and Christians all over this land have been brought to a deep spiritual life and aroused to more active Christian effort for the salvation of others."[19]

But Moody's considered opinion is not the only one worth remembering. Thomas Spurgeon, the son of Moody's cherished friend Charles Spurgeon, captured all that had unfolded as well as anyone. "I love to think," he stated, "that from all parts of the world men came to Chicago to get saved, though they knew it not, and that they went to their distant homes to tell, not so much the wonders of the Fair, as of the great things the Lord had done for them."[20]

THE PATH TO
ROUND TOP

I am over sixty years old. God has showered blessings
upon me. My lot has fallen in very pleasant places.[1]

—D. L. Moody

Out of the Shadow-land, into the sunshine, Cloudless,
eternal, that fades not away.[2]

—Ira Sankey

Four months before, Mr. Moody had planned the
funeral services of his grandchild Irene. . . . As family
and friends followed the white casket borne on a bier
by twelve Mount Hermon students . . . special friends
of the little one, Mr. Moody had remarked to his son,
"That is just as I would want it. No hearse and no
mourning, but just let Mount Hermon boys bear me to
my resting-place."

—*The Life of Dwight L. Moody*

n the morning and evening of Tuesday, February 13, 1898,
D. L. Moody addressed overflow gatherings of students
at Yale University. A third meeting, described by the *New
York Times* as a "monster meeting," was held in the Hyperion
Theatre. There, the *Times* continued, "2,000 were turned away
for lack of room." Students who could not gain entrance to the
hall filled the stairways. At its close, "a delegation from each
class" requested the Yale administration "ask Mr. Moody to
remain several days," or, if that were not possible, "to return to
Yale again in their near future."[3]

Such an event, and the national press it garnered, is testament to Moody's stature as a public figure and his appeal to the
young people of his day. It harkens back as well to a time when
faith was a centerpiece of university life. For all of these reasons, the Yale meetings are important.

Yet these were but a small part of the overall picture of
D. L. Moody's abiding concern for young people. By 1898, the
Northfield schools and the summer conferences held there had
become the central focus of his life. One part gentleman farmer
and one part guiding spirit, he would set out nearly every day in
his pony cart and take a tour of all that was unfolding.

He rejoiced in the sight. As a boy, he had roamed many of
the hills and roads his wagon now traversed—knowing only
hard work, little opportunity, and ever-present poverty. Now,
underprivileged children and young people from all over the
world were being educated and trained for service and ministry.

It was the full flowering of cherished hopes that had their
beginning on the streets of Little Hell long years before in the

slums of Chicago, when he had served in a kind of spiritual triage unit, meeting desperately needy children and their families at points of crisis. Sometimes he could do little more than attend four or five funerals a day, trying to offer some comfort and bring a voice of love, however rough-hewn or untutored, into their lives.[4]

Now, in Northfield, schools had been created where young people could embark on a life the children of Little Hell could never have had. And so, as much as the Yale meetings of 1898 might have meant to Moody, it was the Northfield schools that lay closest to his heart. "They are the best pieces of work I have ever done," he said—telling friends, "I have been able to set in motion streams which will continue long after I have gone."[5]

≈

In 1899, Moody accepted an invitation to conduct a series of meetings in the large Convention Hall of Kansas City in the autumn of that year. Departing Northfield, he started for the west by train on Thursday, November 8.[6] Stopping over in Philadelphia, he was met by his friend John Wanamaker, who "coaxed him very hard to defer his journey as I thought he wasn't very well." But Moody could not be dissuaded.[7] He pushed on to Kansas City.

Arriving in Kansas City on Saturday, November 11, Moody was joined by C. C. Case, a gifted musician who had agreed to conduct the choir during the mission.

Upon arriving at his lodgings at the Coates House, Moody was visited by his old friend Charley Vining. Upon entering

Moody's room, Vining could see that something was wrong. Moody excused himself from rising and remained seated in his chair, saying he was tired.[8] Still, that afternoon he joined Vining and another friend for a drive through the city. He seemed in good spirits, Vining noted, "and joked some, [but] I noticed that he was not himself."[9]

At the Convention Hall on Sunday night, November 12, Moody seemed back in step and "preached with his old fire and spirit."[10] The building was filled to its capacity of fifteen thousand, and several thousand people had to be turned away.[11] Such a cavernous venue might have posed a daunting challenge, but Moody was to strike just the right balance: speaking so as to be heard by all, but "as though he was talking confidentially to a man in the eighth or tenth row."[12] J. Wilbur Chapman recalled:

> The people sat in rapt attention and upon their faces could be traced the effects of varying phases of thought. Toward the close [Mr. Moody] made an appeal, tender as a young mother's love, and unnoticed tears fell from thousands of eyes. In solemn silence, at the last, the benediction dismissed audiences whose souls had been stirred to deepest depths.
>
> The meetings on Monday fulfilled the expectations aroused by Sunday's services. Following the evening sermon an after-meeting was held in the Second Presbyterian Church, just across the street from Convention Hall. The church was crowded, many [were] standing.
>
> As Mr. Moody took his place, the old hymn, "Just as I am," was sung, and then, with no preamble, he began one of

his face to face dealings with inquirers. In a simple, conversational way, he presented the truth, just as though he were sitting by the side of each one before him. He closed with an effective incident from his army experience, illustrating his appeal.

Then [he] paused a moment. The church was still. The ticking of the clock could be distinctly heard. Then he spoke: "Will any one say he will trust Christ? If so, say 'I will.'"

He paused, but no reply came, and then again he put the question quietly, "Who will say he will trust Christ?"

A moment of silence again, and far back in the church there came a low, but firm, response, "I will." At the sound Mr. Moody advanced quickly to the edge of the platform, and with his eyes questioned those before him. The responses came fast and faster, and in a few minutes fully fifty had said "I will."[13]

At breakfast on Tuesday, November 14, C. C. Case saw that Moody looked decidedly unwell:

He looked pale and ate little. I asked how he rested, and he said, "I slept in my chair all night." Of course I knew if he could not lie down he was a sick man. I asked him what was the matter; he said he had had a pain in his chest for a couple of weeks, and added, "I did not let my family know it, for they would not have let me come on here."

I had to urge him for an hour or two before he would consent to call a doctor, but finally he gave in. The doctor put a mustard plaster on his chest, which at once relieved the pain. He preached six sermons after that, but I could see that he was all the time growing weaker, and the last two days he had to be taken to the hall in a carriage, although it was only two blocks away.[14]

Recollections of those who attended the services of the Kansas City outreach reveal many moments that were vintage Moody. He was by turns unconventional, earnest, and pointed. "I have no sympathy with the idea that our best days are behind us," he declared during one service. In another he was at his most compelling: "So many men choose this life on earth, instead of the life in Heaven. Don't close your heart against eternal life. Only take the gift, only take it. Will you do it?"

Finally, one night, he turned to the clergy present on the platform and asked: "Will you ministers allow me to say a word to you?"

"Yes, yes; say what you want," they answered.

"Well," he replied, "I'm not a prophet, but I have a guess to make that I think will prove a true prophecy. You hear so much nowadays about the preacher of the twentieth century. Do you know what sort of a man he will be? He will be the sort of a preacher who opens his Bible and preaches out of that.

"Oh, I'm sick and tired of this essay preaching! I'm nauseated with this 'silver-tongued orator' preaching! I like to hear preachers, and not windmills."[15]

≈

J. Wilbur Chapman remembered that toward noon on Friday, November 17,

Mr. Moody went out driving. He came back thoroughly exhausted. Not until then did he relinquish the hope of preaching that day. He sent for one of the ministers of the committee, Rev. Dr. Matthew S. Hughes, of the Independence Avenue Methodist Episcopal Church, to preach that afternoon, saying, as he made his request, with a flash of his old spirit [and humor], "You Methodists are always prepared to preach."

Mr. Moody told those who were near him that he had never felt so feeble before . . . He had not been able to lie in bed for three nights, but had taken all his rest in his chair, sleeping only a few minutes at a time.

It was decided, upon consultation with his physician, Dr. Schauffler, that he should go home at once. Mr. Moody was sitting in his armchair. He was breathing heavily, and his face seemed puffy and bloated. He said his limbs were swelling, and he had a feeling of oppression about his heart.

"I'm afraid I shall have to give up the meetings," he said. "It's too bad."

He was silent, "It's the first time in forty years of preaching that I have had to give up my meetings."[16]

"Under the imperative order of his physician," Will Moody wrote, "[Father] reluctantly consented to cease work." It was then agreed that he would leave Kansas City that very night on the evening train, traveling "directly home without breaking the journey—which required a day and two nights on the road."[17]

Worrying as Moody's condition was, his return to Northfield was not uneventful. "On the way," Will Moody wrote,

> an incident occurred that cheered and encouraged [Father] greatly. From St. Louis to Detroit the train was delayed by the cleaning out of the locomotive fire grate, and it was feared that connections would be missed at a later point. The new engineer, who was to take the train from Detroit to St. Thomas, learning that Mr. Moody was on the train, returning home sick, sent word to him that he would do his best to make up the lost time.
>
> "Tell him," he said, "that I was converted under him fifteen years ago, and I owe everything to him.[18] I didn't know [his] car was on to-night, but if you want me to make up the time for you I'll do it. Just tell Mr. Moody that one of his friends is on the engine, and then hold your breath."[19] [Thus] the division from Detroit to St. Thomas was covered in the darkness of . . . night at a speed averaging [60 miles per hour], including stops, and the connection for the East was secured.

As a mark of their long friendship, Charles Vining traveled home with Moody. He saw him safely through to Northfield. Almost immediately Vining then prepared to board a train to return to Kansas City. Moody turned to thank him. This done, he paused for a moment, then said: "Tell them they have caged the old lion at last."[20]

Meanwhile, the first indication Moody's family had of his ill-
ness was a tersely worded telegram: "Doctor thinks I need rest.
Am on my way home."

Alighting at the train station, Moody was met and driven
twelve miles to his home. "He went upstairs with little difficulty
to prepare for tea," Will Moody wrote, "but never descended
again. It was hoped that a complete rest would restore [his]
weakened heart, and specialists were consulted who gave
encouragement for an ultimate restoration of health, even if
the old-time vigor could never again return. But day by day
his weakness increased."[21] His beloved wife, Emma, and children, Will, Emma, and Paul, along with Will's wife, May, and
Emma's husband, A. P. Fitt, stayed close to his bedside and kept
a sad vigil. At times they took it in turns, so that someone was
always with him, even through the long hours of the night.

By Thursday, December 21, Moody's health had declined
precipitously. His heart was failing. Nitroglycerin injections
were administered periodically, and these purchased a little
more time. On that day Moody became "rather more nervous
than usual, but nevertheless spoke cheerfully about himself."
Asked if he was comfortable, he said: "Oh, yes! God is very
good to me—and so is my family."[22]

Within a few hours of the end, Moody "fell into a natural
sleep," from which, as Will Moody recalled,

he awoke in about an hour. Suddenly he was heard speaking

in slow and measured words. He was saying: "Earth recedes; Heaven opens before me."

The first impulse was to try to arouse him from what appeared to be a dream.

"No, this is no dream, Will," he replied. "It is beautiful . . . If this is death, it is sweet. There is no valley here. God is calling me, and I must go."[23]

Then, for a time, it "seemed as though he saw beyond the veil." Suddenly, with a strength that belied his condition, he exclaimed: "This is my triumph; this is my coronation day! I have been looking forward to it for years." Joy overtook him. "Dwight! Irene!" he said, calling out the names of the two beloved grandchildren who had died earlier in the year. "I see the children's faces!" Then, thinking he was about to lose consciousness, he spoke again: "Give my love to them all."

It was not long after, Will Moody wrote, "that he 'fell on sleep'—quietly and peacefully."[24]

≈

So many remembered D. L. Moody on the hills of Northfield— preaching on the crest of Round Top—telling students from Harvard and Yale, and students from impoverished homes— African Americans, Native Americans, and students from as far away as Asia—of Christ, the only hope for the world.

Off in the distance were handsome buildings of recent construction, some of the finest academic buildings in America, one European observer commented[25]—but buildings that were, ultimately, but so many handsome means to an end. One could say they were sermons in stone, and as such possessed many compelling stories. He had laid the cornerstone of one building at Northfield with a worn and rusty trowel that had once belonged to his father.[26]

But the sermons Moody preached on Round Top, in no building at all, were what really mattered. As a mason's son, Moody knew that bricks and mortar have their place, and drew forth his gratitude—but they are never what matters most. That honor is reserved for temples of another kind—temples of the human heart, surrendered to God—lives that "preach Christ honestly, faithfully, sincerely and truthfully; holding Him up, not ourselves; exalting Christ."[27]

Moody's family understood, profoundly, that this was why Round Top was so dear to him, and why no better place of final rest could be found. That is why students carried his funeral bier in solemn procession and took him to the crest of the hill one last time. Those who visit his grave can stand there, quietly, and remember another time—hearing, perhaps, echoes of a message he never tired of telling: Christ, the hope of the world.

~

Not long before his death, Moody preached a sermon containing one of his finest word pictures. It was rendered with humor, faith, and a sudden, poetic imagery. There is no better picture of what he was like near the end of his life.

I was down in Texas some time ago, and I happened to pick up a newspaper, and there they called me "Old Moody." Honestly, I never got such a shock from any paper in my life before! I never had been called old before. I went to my hotel, and looked in the looking glass.

My dear friends, I never felt so young in my life as I do to-night; I cannot conceive of getting old. I believe that I have a life that is never going to end. Death may change my position but not my condition, not my standing with Jesus Christ. Death is not going to separate us. That is the teaching of the 8th [Chapter] of Romans.

Old! I wish you all felt as young as I do here to-night. Why, I am only sixty-two years old! If you meet me ten million years hence, then I will be young.[28]

"Why leap ye, ye high hills?" is one of the poems in miniature to be found in the Scriptures. I think of it when I think of Round Top, the high hillside where D. L. and Emma Moody have rested for more than one hundred years.

The entire Connecticut Valley was wreathed in color when my wife, my three-year-old son, and I visited Round Top and Northfield in early October 2009. I don't know that I will ever discover a finer view than the one the crest of Round Top afforded that day.

There was no one else by the graveside, and it was movingly quiet. We knelt in prayer for a few moments and thanked God for the lives and legacy of the Moodys. Then my son, who had waited very patiently, did what he had been wanting to do—roll down the hill.

As I watched him, I thought: *Round Top will leap for very joy when the Lord returns to claim His own to be with Him forever. My little son rolled down the grassy sides of Round Top—laughing—on as beautiful an autumn day as I can ever remember seeing. D. L. Moody would have loved that.*

NOTES

PROLOGUE

1. The descriptor "untouchables" is used by Lyle W. Dorsett in his book *A Passion for Souls: A Life of D. L. Moody* (Chicago: Moody Press, 1997), 74.
2. The names of all the ragged boys pictured in the lithograph depicting them and Moody were: "Red Eye," "Darby the Gobbler," "Smikes," "Butcher," "Kilroy," "Billy Bucktooth," and "Greenhorn." "Madden the Butcher" (seated with a broom on the far right). The boys in the front row are—left to right—"Indian," "Jackie Candles," "Black Stove Pipe," "Sniderick," "Old Man," "Billy Blucorn," "Rag-Breeches Cadet."
3. Elias Nason, *The Lives of . . . Dwight Lyman Moody and Ira David Sankey . . .* (Boston: B. B. Russell, 1877), 68.
4. So far as is known two audio recordings were made of Moody's voice. The recording of Moody reading the Beatitudes dates from 1898, as detailed in the Web article, "D. L. Moody Recording Revealed," posted July 1, 2009 at:

   http://www.moodyministries.net/crp_NewsDetail.aspx?id=39955.

   This article states in part: Only one well-known D. L. Moody recording exists, which is a minute-and-a-half reading of the Beatitudes. However, on Sunday, July 5, a digitally restored version of a second reading begins a sixteen-week series on *Moody Presents* titled "The Hall of Presidents." The two-minute recording arrived on Moody's campus in 1956, but because restoration was needed the audio was archived. It starts with D. L. Moody's strong and booming voice reading the words of Psalm 91: "*He who dwells in the shelter of the Most High will rest in the shadow of the Almighty. I will say of the Lord, 'He is my refuge and my fortress, my God, in whom I trust.'*"

   For a radio broadcast confirming the 1898 date of the Beatitudes recording, see this Web site: http://www.moodyradio.org/moody presents.aspx.

See also D. L. Moody, C. F. Goss, et al, *Echoes from the Pulpit and Platform* (Hartford: Worthington and Co., 1900), 97: "Many of [Mr. Moody's] longer words," C. F. Goss writes, "were terribly shortened, [suffixes] like 'ing' being almost invariably abbreviated [in Yankee fashion] to 'in.' B. F. Jacobs used to say that D. L. Moody was the only man living who could say 'Jerusalem' in two syllables."

5. J. C. Pollock, *Moody* (New York: Macmillan, 1963), 29. The hall was located at the site of what had once been the Old North Market.

6. Ibid., 23.

7. Ibid., 42.

8. Ibid.

9. A figure confirmed by historian Lyle W. Dorsett in his scholarly and authoritative work, *A Passion for Souls* (Chicago: Moody Press, 1997).

Chapter One

1. Gamaliel Bradford, *D. L. Moody: A Worker in Souls* (New York: Doubleday, Doran & Company, 1928), 19. Bradford was described in *Time* magazine as "a wise and searching biographer," and his biography of Moody praised as a "clever, scholarly history." See "Mighty Moody," A Review of Gamaliel Bradford's *D. L. Moody: A Worker in Souls, Time* magazine, Monday, Jan. 16, 1928. Vol. XI No. 3. Posted at: http://www.time.com/time/magazine/article/0,9171,731388,00.html.

2. William R. Moody, *The Life of Dwight L. Moody* (London: Morgan and Scott, 1900), 17.

3. R. B. Cook, *The Life, Work and Sermons of Dwight L. Moody* (Baltimore: R. H. Woodward Company, 1900), 15. Richard Briscoe Cook (1838–1916), D.D., was a British author best known for his biography of Prime Minister William Gladstone, *The Grand Old Man*.

4. D. L. Moody, *The Works of D. L. Moody, Volume 2: Anecdotes* (Chicago: Fleming H. Revell, 1900), 10

5. Moody, Goss, et al, *Echoes from the Pulpit and Platform*, 490–95.

6. J. Wilbur Chapman, *The Life and Work of D. L. Moody* (Philadelphia: International Publishing Co., 1900), 27.

7. D. L. Moody, *The Works of D. L. Moody, Volume 13: Moody's Stories* (New York: Fleming H. Revell, 1899), 18.

8. Chapman, *Life and Work of D. L. Moody*, 46.

9. See W. H. Daniels, *D. L. Moody and His Work* (Hartford: American Publishing Co., 1875), 8; and Chapman, *Life and Work of D. L. Moody*, 45.

10. Paul Moody and A. P. Fitt, *The Shorter Life of D. L. Moody* (Chicago: BICA, 1900), 10.

11. William R. Moody, *The Life of Dwight L. Moody* (New York: Fleming H. Revell, 1900), 20. The copy of this work used for reference throughout this book is housed in the library of Harvard University.

12. Cook, *Life, Work and Sermons of Dwight L. Moody*, 15–17.

13. Daniels, *Moody and His Work*, 9.

14. Ibid., 7. In the preface to his book, Daniels states that he gathered his information "almost entirely from original materials, obtained from first sources [and] by the author in person; who was, for years, a neighbour of Mr. Moody in Chicago, both before and after the great fire."

15. William R. Moody, *The Life of Dwight L. Moody* (London: Morgan and Scott, 1900), 21.

16. Daniels, *Moody and His Work*, 9.

17. Moody, Goss, et al, *Echoes from the Pulpit and Platform*, 601.

18. Ibid.

19. Ibid., 490–95.

20. Ibid.

21. William R. Moody, *D. L. Moody* (New York: Macmillan, 1930), 22.

22. Chapman, *Life and Work of D. L. Moody*, 66.

23. For young Moody's susceptibility to kindness see page 19 of Cook, *Life, Work and Sermons of Dwight L. Moody*.

24. Daniels, *Moody and His Work*, 12–13.

25. Ibid.

26. Ibid., 13–14.

27. Cook, *Life, Work and Sermons of Dwight L. Moody*, 18.

28. Moody, Goss, et al, *Echoes from the Pulpit and Platform*, 34.

29. Daniels, *Moody and His Work*, 13–14.

30. Bradford, *Moody: A Worker in Souls*, 21.

31. Moody, Goss, et al, *Echoes from the Pulpit and Platform*, 35. See also W. R. Moody, *The Life of D. L. Moody* (New York: Fleming H. Revell Company, 1900), 30–31.

32. "[Moody's] total schooling was the equivalent of a fifth-grade education today," from Dr. David Maas, "The Life & Times of D. L. Moody," *Christian History* magazine, January 1, 1990, Issue 25.

33. Chapman, *Life and Work of D. L. Moody*, 52–53.

34. Pollock, *Moody*, 5–6.

35. Moody, Goss, et al, *Echoes from the Pulpit and Platform*, 224–25. Moody's near-drowning must have taken place at this time, since there does not seem to be any other time in his life when he swam so frequently as during his boyhood years. This is an educated guess; but one I think well founded on the accounts of his activities during his teens.

36. William R. Moody, *The Life of D. L. Moody* (New York: Fleming H. Revell Company, 1900), 35.

CHAPTER TWO

1. From the article, "D. L. Moody; A Life of the Great Evangelist—Written by His Son," from the Wednesday, May 19, 1900, edition of the *New York Times*, Saturday Review of Books and Art, page BR16, 785 words.

2. Moody, Goss, et al, *Echoes from the Pulpit and Platform*, 172.

3. Lyle W. Dorsett, *A Passion for Souls: A Life of D. L. Moody* (Chicago: Moody Press, 1997), 42. Here, Dorsett writes, "[Moody] cut a singularly unimpressive figure."

4. *The Autobiography of Benjamin Franklin*, The Harvard Classics, vol. 1 (New York: P.F. Collier & Son Company, 1914).

5. William R. Moody, *The Life of Dwight L. Moody* (London: Morgan & Scott, 1900), 33–34.

6. William R. Moody, *D. L. Moody*, 23.

7. Stanley N. Gundry, *The Wit and Wisdom of D. L. Moody* (Chicago: Moody Press, 1974), 7.

8. See Pollock, *Moody* 7; and H. D. Northrop, *The Life of Labors of Dwight L. Moody...* (Chicago: A.B. Kuhlman Company, 1899), 57. The phrase "no one had been able to slap a saddle on him" is an old New England aphorism for which no attribution is needed.

9. Pollock, *Moody*, 7.

10. Ibid.

11. William R. Moody, *D. L. Moody*, 25–27.

12. This story appears on pages 55–56 of Chapman, *Life and Work of D. L. Moody* (Toronto: The Bradley-Garretson Company, 1900).

13. Dorsett, *Passion for Souls*, 41–42. Here, Dorsett is citing population, immigration, and historical information from the U.S. Census of 1850, Statistics of Massachusetts; Census of 1880, *Social Statistics of Cities*, Boston.

14. D. L. Moody to Brothers, 9 April 1854, Yale Divinity School archives.

15. Ibid.

16. Pollock, *Moody*, 10. Here Pollock writes of Moody's "scant leisure."

17. William R. Moody, *D. L. Moody*, 28–29.

18. Ibid.

19. Ibid.

20. Ibid.

21. Ibid., 30.

22. Pollock, *Moody*, 9.

23. William R. Moody, *D. L. Moody*, 23.

24. Pollock, *Moody*, 9.

25. William R. Moody, *D. L. Moody*, 28.

26. Moody's account of this riot appears in Pollock, *Moody*, 9–10. I have added punctuation and capitalization for ease of understanding.

27. See James D'Wolf Lovett, *Old Town Boston Boys and the Games They Played* (Boston: Privately Printed at the Riverside Press, 1907), 52–53. Here, one old-town Boston boy recalls, "Boys, do you remember those black mince 'slugs,' the turnovers, the hard-tack which we used to soak in the swimming basin and eat while bathing, the spruce beer, and the apple 'dough bats'? The exterior of these last was of a beautiful doughnut brown, and they contained in some part of their depths a trace more or less of apple sauce, like the ring in a cake; one never knew when the prize would be reached, but if it was there we never failed to reach it, and the wonder of it is that all these things tasted so good."

28. Pollock, *Moody*, 10. See also Moody, Goss, et al, *Echoes from the Pulpit and Platform*, 187. Here Moody freely confesses that during his early years in Boston, he swore habitually.

29. Moody's account of this riot appears in Pollock, *Moody*, 10.

30. Ibid.

31. William R. Moody, *D. L. Moody*, 32.

32. Chapman, *Life and Work of D. L. Moody*, 74–75.

33. Ibid.

34. William R. Moody, *The Life of Dwight L. Moody* (New York: Fleming H. Revell, 1900), 40.

35. Kimball's account appears in Chapman, *Life and Work of D. L. Moody*, 75–76.

36. Chapman, *Life and Work of D. L. Moody*, 75–76.

37. William R. Moody, *Life of Dwight L. Moody*, 42.

CHAPTER THREE

1. D. L. Moody, as quoted on page 18 of J.C. Pollock, *Moody*, (New York: Macmillan, 1963).

2. D. L. Moody, *Secret Power* (New York: Fleming H. Revell Company, 1881), 97.

3. Dorsett, *A Passion to Save Souls*, 61.

4. William R. Moody, *Life of Dwight L. Moody*, 75.

5. Moody, *Secret Power*, 65–66.

6. From Sean Wilentz's book, *Chants Democratic: New York City and the Rise of American Working Class, 1788–1850*, 20th edition (New York: Oxford University Press, 2004).

7. Had he achieved his goal of amassing a fortune of one hundred thousand dollars, it would have been a sum 332 times the average annual income of a tradesman. If a tradesman were to work fifty years at the 1850 wage, Moody's one hundred thousand dollars would be almost seven times the lifetime earnings of a tradesman—a truly enormous sum—KCB.

8. William R. Moody, *Life of Dwight L. Moody*, 75.

9. Both letters as quoted on page 16 of Pollock, *Moody*.

10. William R. Moody, *Life of Dwight L. Moody*, 46.

11. Pollock, *Moody*, 17.

12. Paul Moody and A. P. Fitt, *The Shorter Life of D. L. Moody* (Chicago: BICA, 1900), 23.

13. Ibid., 24.

14. Ibid., 25.

15. Moody, Goss, et al, *Echoes from the Pulpit and Platform*, 38.

16. Moody and Fitt, *Shorter Life of D. L. Moody*, 23.
17. Ibid., 25.
18. Ibid.
19. As quoted on page 23 of Pollock, *Moody*.
20. Pollock, *Moody*, 43.
21. Ibid., 24.
22. Ibid., 25.
23. The information related in the foregoing four paragraphs is gleaned from Pollock, *Moody*, 25–26.
24. As quoted in G. T. B. Davis, *Dwight L. Moody: The Man and His Mission* (K. T. Boland, 1900).
25. As quoted in Pollock, *Moody*, 26.
26. Ibid.
27. Dorsett, *A Passion for Souls*, 65–66.
28. Ibid.
29. i.e., quarantine zone.
30. W. H. Daniels, *D. L. Moody and His Work*, new edition, revised (Hartford: American Publishing Company, 1877), 34. Daniels's reference to the "Five Points" section of New York City is a reminder of the squalor and violence depicted in the Martin Scorsese film *The Gangs of New York*. This casts a vivid light on the conditions Moody encountered in the "Little Hell" section of Chicago.
31. Daniels, *Moody and His Work*, new edition, revised, 37. As quoted in Dorsett, *A Passion for Souls*, 67–68.
32. Dorsett, *A Passion for Souls*, 65.
33. This story appears in the January 2, 1862, edition of the *Chicago Tribune*, and is quoted in William R. Moody, *D. L. Moody* (New York: Macmillan Company, 1930), 70.
34. William R. Moody, *The Life of Dwight L. Moody* (Chicago: Fleming H. Revell, 1900), 76–77.

CHAPTER FOUR

1. L. T. Remlap, ed., *"The Gospel awakening." Comprising the sermons and addresses, prayer-meeting talks and Bible readings of the great revival meetings conducted by Moody and Sankey*, 20th ed. (Chicago: Fairbanks and Palmer Publishing Co., 1885), 75–76.

2. The information in this paragraph and the ones that follow concerning Moody's Civil War work with the Christian Commission are taken from *The Dictionary of American Biography*, vol. 7, ed. by Dumas Malone (New York: Charles Scribner's Sons, 1962), 103.

3. As quoted in *The Dictionary of American Biography* (New York: Charles Scribner's Sons, 1962), 103.

4. See *The Dictionary of American Biography*, 103.

5. This quote and information about Moody's wartime service is taken from pages 43–45 of Pollock, *Moody*.

6. Pollock, *Moody*, 45. Note: The spelling, spacing, and grammar errors are from Moody's original letter and retained as is to give the most faithful flavor to this time of Moody's life.—KCB.

7. Information supplied by the National Park Service and posted on the Web site for Ken Burns's miniseries *The Civil War* at: http://www.pbs.org/civilwar/war/map4.html.

8. Ibid.

9. Moody, Goss, et al, *Echoes from the Pulpit and Platform*, 164–66.

10. Ibid., 45.

11. Ibid., 224.

CHAPTER FIVE

1. From the poem "A Metrical Essay," by Oliver Wendell Holmes Sr., first read publicly at Harvard University in August 1836.

2. A descriptor applied to T. R. by his distinguished biographer, Edmund Morris, in his introduction to *The Seven Worlds of Theodore Roosevelt*, by Edward Wagenknecht, p. x.

3. Pollock, *Moody*, 67–68.

4. Ibid., 24.

5. Ibid., 27.

6. Ibid., 24.

7. Ibid., 29.

8. Ibid., 28.

9. As quoted on page 29 of Pollock, *Moody*.

10. Pollock, *Moody*, 48.

11. Ibid.

12. Ibid.

13. Ibid.

Chapter Six

1. Edward Young, *The Poetical Works of Edward Young*, Vol. 1 (London; Bell and Daldy, n.d.), 253.
2. As quoted on page 74 of Pollock, *Moody*.
3. Charles Morris, ed., *Famous Orators of the World and Their Best Orations* (Philadelphia: The John C. Winston Co., 1902), 290.
4. Ibid.
5. L. T. Remlap, ed., *"The Gospel awakening." Comprising the sermons and addresses, prayer-meeting talks and Bible readings of the great revival meetings conducted by Moody and Sankey*, 20th ed. (Chicago: Fairbanks and Palmer Publishing Co., 1885), 66–67.
6. J. B. McClure, ed., *Anecdotes and Illustrations of D. L. Moody* (Chicago: Rhodes & McClure, 1878), 7–9.
7. Remlap, ed., *"The Gospel awakening,"* 67–68. Italics added.
8. Pollock, *Moody*, 70.
9. Ibid.
10. Ibid., 74. Here, Pollock makes an important distinction regarding Moody and the influence of the Plymouth Brethren: "Harry Morehouse was of the Plymouth Brethren. Moody never denied their influence [and] eagerly bought their commentaries. [But] his common sense kept him from selling out to theories or speculative allegories that the married [the Brethren's] attempts to allow Scripture to interpret Scripture, and he had no truck with the separatist tendencies of some of them, 'eating gingerbread all by themselves in a corner,' as he expressed it. In his relations with the Brethren, Moody showed his knack of drawing strength from a movement without becoming its slave." Presumably, Harry Morehouse avoided the less praiseworthy excesses of some among the Brethren as well.
11. Ibid., 70.
12. William Wilberforce, as quoted on page 75 of Robert and Samuel Wilberforce, *The Life of William Wilberforce*, vol. 1 (London: John Murray, 1838).
13. As quoted on page 74 of Pollock, *Moody*.
14. Moody, Goss, et al, *Echoes from the Pulpit and Platform*, 252.

15. Sam Paxton, compiler, *Short Quotations of D. L. Moody* (Chicago: Moody Press, 1961), 37.
16. From the introduction to Henry Drummond's *The Greatest Thing in the World* (New York: Fleming H. Revell Company, 1898).

CHAPTER SEVEN

1. *The Burning of Chicago: Poems of the Great Chicago Fire*, collected by Francis J. Gerty (Chicago: The Hendricks School Press, 1915).
2. William R. Moody, *The Life of Dwight L. Moody* (Chicago: Fleming H. Revell, 1900), 117.
3. Dorsett, *A Passion for Souls*, 151. Here the commonplace nature of fires in Chicago is referenced.
4. This summary account of Moody's actions before and during the Great Chicago Fire comes from Moody, Goss, et al, *Echoes from the Pulpit and Platform*, 173–74.
5. The summary given in the proceeding four paragraphs is based upon information found in Pollock, *Moody*, 87.
6. The summary given in the preceding five paragraphs is based upon information found in Pollock, *Moody*, 88.
7. Moody, Goss, et al, *Echoes from the Pulpit and Platform*, 173—74.
8. H. D. Northrop, *The Life and Labors of Dwight L. Moody* (Chicago: A. B. Kuhlman Company, 1899), 332.
9. William R. Moody, *The Life of Dwight L. Moody* (Chicago: Fleming H. Revell, 1900), 145–46.
10. D. L. Moody, *The Works of D. L. Moody, Volume 2: Anecdotes* (Chicago: Fleming H. Revell, 1900), 76.
11. Moody, Goss, et al, *Echoes from the Pulpit and Platform*, 55.
12. Ibid., 56.
13. This time of crisis has been best described by Dorsett in *A Passion of Souls*, 156.
14. As quoted in David McCullough, *Mornings on Horseback* (New York: Simon and Schuster, 1981), 15.
15. Moody, Goss, et al, *Echoes from the Pulpit and Platform*, 85. "It is no uncommon thing in life," Goss writes, "to see [that] men of such extraordinary . . . endowments [are] cold, hard, just, and unloving. But *tears start to the eyes of those who knew Mr. Moody well, at the thought of*

the absolutely inexhaustible depths of his love for all living things. Horses, dogs, cows, animals, and birds—all excited the emotions of his heart."

And again, on page 86: "[Mr. Moody] was in Cincinnati when the news of [Henry] Drummond's death came, and that evening at my table he laid his knife and fork down and cried like a child. 'He was the most Christ-like man I ever met. I never saw a fault in him,' he said over and over again through his sobs."

16. From *Holding the Fort: comprising sermons and addresses at the Great Revival meetings conducted by Moody and Sankey*, by M. Laird Simons (Norwich, Connecticut: Henry Bill Publishing Co., 1877).

17. Moody and Fitt, *The Shorter Life of D. L. Moody*, 67.

18. Ibid.

19. From *Holding the Fort: comprising sermons and addresses at the Great Revival meetings conducted by Moody and Sankey*, by M. Laird Simons.

CHAPTER EIGHT

1. As quoted on page 104 of Pollock, *Moody*.
2. As quoted on page 101 of Pollock, *Moody*.
3. Pollock, *Moody*, 101.
4. Ibid.
5. As quoted on page 172 of Dorsett, *A Passion for Souls*.
6. Dorsett, *A Passion for Souls*, 177.
7. Ibid.
8. Ibid.
9. Pollock, *Moody*, 103.
10. Ibid., 104.
11. Ibid.
12. Ibid.
13. For the purpose of narrative flow, I have slightly paraphrased Bennett's response to Moody as recounted on page 104 of Pollock, *Moody*.
14. W. R. Moody, *D. L. Moody*, 301.
15. Pollock, *Moody*, 105.
16. W. R. Moody, *The Life of Dwight L. Moody* (Chicago: Fleming H. Revell, 1900), 156.
17. The account of this brief conversation appears in Pollock, *Moody*, 105–6.

18. Pollock, *Moody*, 106.
19. Ibid.
20. All of the information in this paragraph, including the quote therein, is taken from Pollock, *Moody*, 106.
21. W. R. Moody, *The Life of Dwight L. Moody*, 156.
22. All of the information in this paragraph is taken from Pollock, *Moody*, 106.
23. Ibid.
24. W. R. Moody, *The Life of Dwight L. Moody*, 160.
25. Ibid.
26. Ibid., 160–61.
27. Ibid., 161.
28. Ibid.
29. Ibid., 161–62.
30. Ibid., 162.
31. Ibid.
32. Ibid., 163.
33. Ibid.
34. Ibid., 164.
35. Ibid.

CHAPTER NINE

1. W. R. Moody, *The Life of Dwight L. Moody*, 165.
2. The information regarding places Moody and Sankey held meetings in after Sunderland is taken from Dorsett, *A Passion for Souls*, 186.
3. W. R. Moody, *The Life of Dwight L. Moody*, 189.
4. Ibid.
5. Ibid., 189–90.
6. Ibid.
7. All the information in this paragraph, including the quote therein, is taken from W. R. Moody, *The Life of Dwight L. Moody*, 190.
8. W. R. Moody, *The Life of Dwight L. Moody*, 190.
9. Ibid., 197.
10. Ibid.
11. Ibid.
12. Ibid., 197–98.

13. Ibid., 198–99.

14. Ibid., 199.

15. Ibid.

16. Ibid., 199–200.

17. All the information in this paragraph, including the quote therein, is taken from Pollock, *Moody*, 144.

18. All the information in this paragraph is taken from Pollock, *Moody*, 144.

19. All the information in this paragraph, including the quote therein, is taken from Pollock, *Moody*, 144.

20. Ibid., 145.

21. Pollock, *Moody*, 145.

22. W. R. Moody, *The Life of Dwight L. Moody*, 170.

23. Ibid.

24. Ibid.

25. Ibid., 171–72. To determine what this amount is in today's dollars, one must multiply by a factor of 8.

26. W. R. Moody, *The Life of Dwight L. Moody*, 172.

27. All the information in this paragraph, including the quote therein, is taken from W. R. Moody, *The Life of Dwight L. Moody*, 172.

28. W. R. Moody, *The Life of Dwight L. Moody*, 173.

29. Ibid.

30. Ibid.

31. Ibid., 173–74.

32. To determine what this amount is in today's dollars, one must multiply by a factor of 8. This results in a figure of $2,859,109.12.

33. W. R. Moody, *The Life of Dwight L. Moody*, 174.

34. All the information in this paragraph, including the quote therein, is taken from W. R. Moody, *The Life of Dwight L. Moody*, 174.

35. W. R. Moody, *The Life of Dwight L. Moody*, 174–75.

36. Ibid., 251.

Chapter Ten

1. Chapman, *Life and Work of D. L. Moody*, 35.

2. Ibid., 42–43.

3. The paragraphs that follow concerning the origin of the Northfield

Seminary are paraphrased from W. R. Moody, *The Life of Dwight L. Moody*, 319–24.

4. W. R. Moody, *The Life of Dwight L. Moody*, 320.
5. Ibid.
6. Ibid.
7. W. R. Moody, *D. L. Moody*, 301.
8. W. R. Moody, *The Life of Dwight L. Moody*, 321.
9. Ibid.
10. Ibid., 322.
11. All the information about the curriculum of the Northfield Seminary is taken from W. R. Moody, *The Life of Dwight L. Moody*, 322.
12. Ibid., 323.
13. All the information in this paragraph is taken from W. R. Moody, *The Life of Dwight L. Moody*, 323.
14. All the information in this paragraph, including the quotes therein, is taken from W. R. Moody, *The Life of Dwight L. Moody*, 323.
15. Ibid.

Chapter Eleven

1. Moody, Goss, et al, *Echoes from the Pulpit and Platform*, 77.
2. W. R. Moody, *The Life of Dwight L. Moody*, 327.
3. All the information in this paragraph, including the quotes therein, is taken from W. R. Moody, *The Life of Dwight L. Moody*, 327.
4. Ibid., 327–28.
5. All the information in this paragraph, including the quotes therein, is taken from W. R. Moody, *The Life of Dwight L. Moody*, 328.
6. Ibid.
7. Ibid.
8. Ibid., 328–29.
9. W. R. Moody, *The Life of Dwight L. Moody*, 329.
10. All the information in this paragraph, including the quotes therein, is taken from W. R. Moody, *The Life of Dwight L. Moody*, 329.
11. Ibid.
12. Ibid., 330.
13. Ibid.
14. Ibid., 330, 333.

15. A paraphrase of Luke 12:48 (NASB): "From everyone who has been given much, much will be required."

16. W. R. Moody, *The Life of Dwight L. Moody*, 333.

17. Ibid.

18. Ibid.

19. Ibid.

20. Ibid., 334–35.

21. Ibid., 335–36.

22. Ibid., 336.

CHAPTER TWELVE

1. General background information posted online by the Moody Bible Institute, accessed on 20 October 2009. See:
http://www.moodyministries.net/crp_MainPage.aspx?id=62.

2. All of the biographical information about Emma Dryer in this paragraph is taken from a summary of her life given by Dorsett in his book *A Passion for Souls*, 165–66.

3. All of the biographical information about Emma Dryer in this paragraph, including the quote from Emma Dryer, is taken from a summary of her life given by Dorsett in his book *A Passion for Souls*, 166.

4. All of the biographical information about Emma Dryer in this paragraph is taken from a summary of her life given by Dorsett in his book *A Passion for Souls*, 166.

5. Ibid.

6. Robert Isaac and Samuel Wilberforce, *The Life of William Wilberforce*, vol. 3, (London: John Murray, 1838), 374.

7. All of the biographical information about Emma Dryer in this paragraph is taken from a summary of her life given by Dorsett in his book *A Passion for Souls*, 168.

8. All of the biographical information about Emma Dryer in this paragraph, including the quote from Daniels, is taken from a summary of her life given by Dorsett in his book *A Passion for Souls*, 168.

9. See W. H. Daniels, ed., *Moody, His Words, Work and Workers* (Hartford: American Publishing Co., 1875), 503–04.

10. General background information posted on online by the Moody Bible Institute, accessed on 20 October 2009. See:
http://www.moodyministries.net/crp_MainPage.aspx?id=62.

11. Ibid.
12. General background information, including the quote from D. L. Moody, posted online by the Moody Bible Institute, and accessed on 20 October 2009. See:
http://www.moodyministries.net/crp_MainPage.aspx?id=62.
13. This mission statement quote is part of an article posted online by the Moody Bible Institute, accessed on 20 October 2009 at:
http://www.moodyministries.net/crp_MainPage.aspx?id=790.

CHAPTER THIRTEEN

1. Moody, Goss, et al, *Echoes from the Pulpit and Platform*, 4.
2. R. P. T. Coffin, "A Review of Paul D. Moody's *My Father: An Intimate Portrait of Dwight Moody*," in Book Talk: A Review of New England Books, a column in the May 1938 issue of *Yankee* magazine, May 1938, 36.
3. Ibid.
4. Ibid.
5. Ibid.
6. As quoted in Stanley and Patricia Gundry, eds., *The Wit and Wisdom of D. L. Moody* (Chicago: Moody Press, 1974), 43.
7. Coffin, "A Review of Paul D. Moody's *My Father*," 36.
8. Ibid., 37.
9. Ibid.
10. A point well made by Goss in his biographical sketch of Moody in Moody, Goss, et al, *Echoes from the Pulpit and Platform*, 58. Here Goss speaks of Moody and Sankey "battling with the hoary customs and prejudices of the past" during their first great evangelistic campaign in Britain in 1872.
11. Cook, *Life, Work and Sermons of Dwight L. Moody*, 200.
12. Moody, *Secret Power*, 40–41.
13. A. T. Pierson, *Evangelistic Work in Principle and Practice* (New York: Baker and Taylor, 1887), 252.
14. William R. Moody, *The Life of Dwight L. Moody*, 240–41.
15. Moody, Goss, et al, *Echoes from the Pulpit and Platform*, 97.
16. D. L. Moody, *The Works of D. L. Moody, Volume 2: Anecdotes* (Chicago: Fleming H. Revell, 1900), preface. Italics added.

17. *The New York Weekly Witness* newspaper, *Ten Days with D. L. Moody* (New York: J. S. Ogilvie and Company, 1886), 102.
18. Ibid., 77–78.
19. Ibid.
20. Ibid., 81.
21. D. L. Moody, *Twelve Select Sermons* (Chicago: Fleming H. Revell, 1884), 39.
22. Ibid., 42.
23. Ibid., 1.
24. Ibid., 31.
25. Ibid., 31–32.
26. Ibid., 35–36.
27. From the article "D. L. Moody; A Life of the Great Evangelist—Written by His Son," from the Wednesday, May 19, 1900, edition of the *New York Times*, Saturday Review of Books and Art, Page BR16, 785 words.
28. Ibid.
29. Michael A. Tatem, "A Review of *Commending the Faith: The Preaching of D. L. Moody*," Journal of the Evangelical Theological Society, March 2002.

CHAPTER FOURTEEN

1. "The Spree's Great Peril; The Steamer Saved By Her Water-Tight Compartments. Towed Into Queenstown With A Broken Shaft And A Hole In Her Bottom—A Panic Among Her Passengers—One Man Jumped Overboard In His Fright," an article appearing on page 1 of the December 4, 1892, edition of the *New York Times*, accessed on 9 July 2009 at the Web site: http://query.nytimes.com/gst/abstract.html?res=9405E3DF1731E033A25757C0A9649D94639ED7CF.
2. Dorsett, *A Passion for Souls*, 363.
3. Moody and Fitt, *The Shorter Life of D. L. Moody*, 99–100.
4. H. B. Hartzler, *Moody in Chicago, or, The World Fair Gospel Campaign* (New York: Fleming H. Revell, 1894), 199.
5. Moody and Fitt, *The Shorter Life of D. L. Moody*, 100.
6. Dorsett, *A Passion for Souls*, 363.

7. *The Autobiography of Oliver Otis Howard*, vol. 2 (New York: The Baker & Taylor Company, 1907), 559.

8. Moody and Fitt, *The Shorter Life of D. L. Moody*, 100–1.

9. Ibid., 101.

10. *The Autobiography of Oliver Otis Howard*, vol. 2 (New York: The Baker & Taylor Company, 1907), 561–62.

11. Moody and Fitt, *The Shorter Life of D. L. Moody*, 101–2.

12. Ibid., 102–3.

13. Ibid., 103–4.

14. Ibid., 104.

CHAPTER FIFTEEN

1. H. B. Hartzler, *Moody in Chicago, or, The World's Fair Gospel Campaign* (New York: Fleming H. Revell, 1894), 70–71.

2. From the 2,727-word article "Moody's Spirit Marches Forward," by L. H. Robbins in the Sunday, January 31, 1937, issue of *The New York Times Magazine*.

3. Dorsett, *A Passion for Souls*, 391.

4. William R. Moody, *The Life of Dwight L. Moody*, 409.

5. Moody and Fitt, *The Shorter Life of D. L. Moody*, 96.

6. As stated in A. J. Liebling, *Chicago: The Second City* (Lincoln, Nebraska: Bison Books—University of Nebraska Press, 2004).

7. Matthew 23:37—from the New International Version of the Bible. The profound symbolism of Moody's being in Jerusalem when he realized the need for a Christian outreach at the World Fair was first written about by William R. Moody on page 409 of *The Life of Dwight L. Moody*.

8. William R. Moody, *The Life of Dwight L. Moody*, 410.

9. Ibid., 413.

10. Dorsett, *A Passion for Souls*, 391.

11. Ibid. Dorsett reports that nearly $800 a day needed to be raised for Moody and his coworkers to cover expenses. Rounding this number up to 800, and multiplying by 180 days (the six months that Moody and his colleagues were active), one arrives at the sum of $144,000 in 1893 dollars. The conversion rate to 2007 dollars is secured by multiplying by a factor of 8, thus arriving at figure just under 1.2 million dollars.

Allowing for two more years to 2009, the figure of 1.2 million is most reasonable.

12. Dorsett, *A Passion for Souls*, 391.
13. Pollock, *Moody*, 283.
14. Dorsett, *A Passion for Souls*, 391.
15. As quoted on page 284 of Pollock, *Moody*.
16. Pollock, *Moody*, 284.
17. Ibid., 283.
18. William R. Moody, *The Life of Dwight L. Moody*, 420.
19. As quoted in Dorsett, *A Passion for Souls*, 391.
20. Ibid.

Chapter Sixteen

1. Moody, Goss, et al, *Echoes from the Pulpit and Platform*, 155–56.
2. A. W. Williams, *The Life and Work of Dwight L. Moody* (Philadelphia: P.W. Ziegler and Co., 1900), 344.
3. From "Mr. Moody Defends Yale: Holds Crowded Meetings There," a 483-word article published on page 7 of the Wednesday, February 14, 1898, issue of the *New York Times*.
4. D. L. Moody, *To the Work, To the Work: Exhortations to Christians* (Chicago: Fleming H. Revell, 1884), 128–31.
5. William R. Moody, *The Life of Dwight L. Moody*, 319–20.
6. Ibid., 545.
7. Pollock, *Moody*, 312.
8. Ibid., 313.
9. Ibid.
10. Ibid.
11. Chapman, *The Life and Work of D. L. Moody*, 263.
12. Pollock, *Moody*, 313.
13. Chapman, *The Life and Work of D. L. Moody*, 263–64.
14. William R. Moody, *The Life of Dwight L. Moody*, 545.
15. Ibid., 547–48.
16. Chapman, *The Life of Work of D. L. Moody*, 266–67.
17. William R. Moody, *The Life of Dwight L. Moody*, 548–49.
18. Ibid., 549.
19. Chapman, *The Life and Work of D. L. Moody*, 268.

20. Ibid.

21. William R. Moody, *The Life of Dwight L. Moody*, 549–50.

22. Ibid., 551.

23. Ibid., 552.

24. Ibid., 552–53.

25. Chapman, *The Life and Work of D. L. Moody* (Philadelphia: International Publishing Co., 1900), 44. Here Chapman writes: "Henry Drummond describes somewhere his first astonishment at finding this little New England hamlet with a dozen of the finest educational buildings in America, and of his surprise when he stopped to think that all these buildings owed their existence to a man whose name is perhaps associated in the minds of three-fourths of his countrymen, not with education, but with the want of it."

26. See *My Life and the Story of the Gospel Hymns by Ira D. Sankey* (New York: Harper & Brothers, 1907), 24.

27. Moody, *Secret Power*, 58.

28. D. L. Moody, *The Works of D. L. Moody, Volume 14: Latest Sermons* (Chicago: Fleming H. Revell, 1900), 43.

SELECTED
BIBLIOGRAPHY

Bradford, Gamaliel. *D. L. Moody: A Worker in Souls*. New York: Doubleday, Doran & Company, 1928.

Chapman, J. Wilbur. *The Life and Work of D. L. Moody*. Philadelphia: International Publishing Co., 1900.

Chapman, *Life and Work of D. L. Moody*. Toronto: The Bradley-Garretson Company, 1900.

Cook, R. B. *The Life, Work and Sermons of Dwight L. Moody*. Baltimore: R. H. Woodward Company, 1900.

Daniels, W. H. *D. L. Moody and His Work*, new edition, revised. Hartford: American Pub. Co., 1877.

Daniels, W. H. *D. L. Moody and His Work*. Hartford: American Publishing Co., 1875.

Daniels, W. H., ed. *Moody, His Words, Work and Workers*. Hartford: American Pub. Co., 1875.

Davis, G. T. B. *Dwight L. Moody: The Man and His Mission*. K. T. Boland, 1900.

Dorsett, Lyle W. *A Passion for Souls*. Chicago: Moody Press, 1997.

Drummond, Henry. *The Greatest Thing in the World*. New York: Fleming H. Revell Company, 1898.

Gerty, Francis J. *The Burning of Chicago: Poems of the Great Chicago Fire*. Chicago: The Hendricks School Press, 1915.

Gundry, Stanley and Patricia, eds., *The Wit and Wisdom of D. L. Moody*. Chicago: Moody Press, 1974.

Hartzler, H. B. *Moody in Chicago, or, The World Fair Gospel Campaign*. New York: Fleming H. Revell, 1894.

Isaac, Robert and Samuel Wilberforce. *The Life of William Wilberforce*, vols. 1 and 3. London: John Murray, 1838.

Liebling, A. J. *Chicago: The Second City*. Lincoln, Nebraska: Bison Books—University of Nebraska Press, 2004.

Lovett, James D'Wolf. *Old Town Boston Boys and the Games They Played*. Boston: Privately Printed at the Riverside Press, 1907.

Malone, Dumas, ed. *The Dictionary of American Biography*, vol. 7. New York: Charles Scribner's Sons, 1962.

McClure, J. B., ed., *Anecdotes and Illustrations of D. L. Moody*. Chicago: Rhodes & McClure, 1878.

McCullough, David. *Mornings on Horseback*. New York: Simon and Schuster, 1981.

Moody, D. L. and C. F. Goss, et al, *Echoes from the Pulpit and Platform*. Hartford: Worthington and Co., 1900.

Moody, D. L. *Secret Power*. New York: Fleming H. Revell Company, 1881.

Moody, D. L. *The Works of D. L. Moody, Volumes 2, 13, 14*. New York: Fleming H. Revell, 1899–1900.

Moody, D. L. *To the Work, To the Work: Exhortations to Christians*. Chicago: Fleming H. Revell, 1884.

Moody, D. L. *Twelve Select Sermons*. Chicago: Fleming H. Revell, 1884.

Moody, Paul and A. P. Fitt, *The Shorter Life of D. L. Moody*. Chicago: BICA, 1900.

Moody, William R. *D. L. Moody*. New York: Macmillan, 1930.

Moody, William R. *The Life of Dwight L. Moody*. Chicago: Fleming H. Revell, 1900.

Moody, William R. *The Life of Dwight L. Moody*. London: Morgan & Scott, 1900.

Moody, William R. *The Life of Dwight L. Moody*. New York: Fleming H. Revell, 1900.

Morris, Charles, ed. *Famous Orators of the World and Their Best Orations*. Philadelphia: The John C. Winston Co., 1902.

My Life and the Story of the Gospel Hymns by Ira D. Sankey. New York: Harper & Brothers, 1907.

Nason, Elias. *The Lives of . . . Dwight Lyman Moody and Ira David Sankey*. Boston: B. B. Russell, 1877.

Northrop, H. D. *The Life and Labors of Dwight L. Moody*. Chicago: A. B. Kuhlman Company, 1899.

Paxton, Sam, compiler, *Short Quotations of D. L. Moody*. Chicago: Moody Press, 1961.

Pierson, A. T. *Evangelistic Work in Principle and Practice*. New York: Baker and Taylor, 1887.

Remlap, L. T., ed. *"The Gospel awakening." Comprising the sermons and addresses, prayer-meeting talks and Bible readings of the great revival meetings conducted by Moody and Sankey*, 20th ed. Chicago: Fairbanks and Palmer Publishing Co., 1885.

Simons, M. Laird. *Holding the Fort: comprising sermons and addresses at the Great Revival meetings conducted by Moody and Sankey*. Norwich, Connecticut: Henry Bill Publishing Co., 1877.

The Autobiography of Benjamin Franklin, The Harvard Classics, vol. 1. New York: P. F. Collier & Son Company, 1914.

The Autobiography of Oliver Otis Howard, vol. 2. New York: The Baker & Taylor Company, 1907.

The New York Weekly Witness newspaper, *Ten Days with D. L. Moody*. New York: J. S. Ogilvie and Company, 1886.

Wilentz, Sean. *Chants Democratic: New York City and the Rise of American Working Class, 1788–1850*, 20th edition. New York: Oxford University Press, 2004.

Williams, A. W. *The Life and Work of Dwight L. Moody*. Philadelphia: P. W. Ziegler and Co., 1900.

Young, Edward. *The Poetical Works of Edward Young*, Vol. 1. London; Bell and Daldy, n.d.

ACKNOWLEDGMENTS

I wish to say at the outset that I owe a great debt to John Pollock, who, in the very early stages of my research for this book, wrote me a letter about D. L. Moody and his own research nearly fifty years ago. It is chief among the many Moody-related treasures I now possess—a close second being a first printing of his masterly biography *Moody* (Macmillan, 1963). Both the letter and the book helped me get to know D. L. Moody in a way that made me want to know more.

I wish to thank Joel Miller, vice president at Thomas Nelson, for extending the invitation to write this book as part of the Christian Encounters series. He and his colleagues have made every aspect of the publishing process a pleasure, as has my agent, Bucky Rosenbaum. Both Joel and Bucky have believed in this project from the first time I spoke of it. My debt to them in this regard is profound.

Before I ever visited Northfield, I saw Moody's birthplace and home through dozens of one-hundred-year-old postcards that I purchased from one of New England's finest antiquarian bookstores, DeWolfe and Wood of Alfred, Maine. I prize these glimpses of yesteryear, as they led me to undertake a visit to Northfield with my wife, Kelly, and son, Sam, that I shall always remember.

Lastly, I wish to pay tribute to the memory of D. L. Moody

himself. I don't know when I have ever encountered someone who was more vibrantly alive. "Love is the lever," he said, "with which Christ lifts the world." How we need that message today, even as we need to renew our acquaintance with a man who should always be a living part of our cultural memory—a man who always strove to love fully, richly and deeply.